Dear Tim and C

CONQUERING THE DRAGON

God Bless,

Shalom,

Kimon

CONQUERING THE DRAGON

The true life story of a former triad gang member

Kim Goh
with
Andrew Chamberlain

Authentic

MILTON KEYNES ● COLORADO SPRINGS ● HYDERABAD

14 13 12 11 10 09 08   8 7 6 5 4 3 2 1

First published 2008 by Authentic Media
9 Holdom Avenue, Bletchley, Milton Keynes, MK1 1QR, UK
1820 Jet Stream Drive, Colorado Springs, CO 80921, USA
OM Authentic Media, Medchal Road, Jeedimetla Village,
Secunderabad 500 055, A.P., India
www.authenticmedia.co.uk

Authentic Media is a division of IBS-STL U.K., limited by guarantee, with its
Registered Office at Kingstown Broadway, Carlisle, Cumbria CA3 0HA.
Registered in England & Wales No. 1216232. Registered charity 270162

British Library Cataloguing in Publication Data
A catalogue record for this book is available from the British Library

ISBN-13: 978-1-86024-616-6

Cover Design by David Lund
Print Management by Adare Carwin
Printed in Great Britain by J.H. Haynes & Co., Sparkford

Contents

Acknowledgements

This book covers my journey in life, with various people participating and influencing its making.

Most of all I owe everything to God, my Heavenly Father, for reaching out to a lost, sinful soul and giving me a wonderful gift in his Son, Jesus Christ.

Next I want to thank my wife, Mary, for her love. She is my best supporter, trusted friend, and most honest critic. She brings wisdom, inspiration and challenge into my life of service in God's kingdom.

I am also thankful to my friends and mentors who nurtured me in my faith, especially the late Revd Mark Kellett, Revd Dr William Davies, Revd Dr Eric Rogers, Revd Dr Howard Mellor, the late Revd Dr Rob Frost, Revd Martyn Atkins, Roger and Margaret Hoyle, John Hunt, Dr John Aston and Revd Dr Lorna Khoo (Singapore).

I am grateful to my brother in Christ, Andrew Chamberlain, who is my co-writer for this book, and without whose help this book would not have been possible.

Finally, thank you to Malcolm Down and the team at Authentic Media for your interest, enthusiasm and faith in the production of the book.

1

Russian Roulette

When the British ruled Hong Kong, all Chinese secret societies were seen as a criminal threat and together defined as 'triads' . . . The name of the 'Three Harmonies Society' (the 'Sanhehui' grouping of the Tiandihui) is in fact the source of the term 'Triad' that has become synonymous with Chinese organized crime.

Wikipedia

If a man points a gun at you once, you could be forgiven for getting upset with him. If he does it again, maybe one of you has to die.

That was my conclusion as I played Russian roulette with a guy called Ronnie on a dusty road outside Brunswick, Ohio. I'd had a few skirmishes with Ronnie in the past, and this time I thought perhaps one of us really would die.

Ronnie was a twitchy character with too much pride for his own good. Half hippy, half gangster, he swaggered around simply to hide his own fear. He was swaggering now as he walked towards me, revolver in hand. I can't say I was surprised when he pulled the gun; we had been working up to this moment for months.

You are so frightened of death, I thought, *so full of bravado, like all cowards.*

1

When we first met, Ronnie took an instant dislike to me, referring to me as 'Tokyo Joe'. I am actually of Chinese descent and originally from Singapore; but that didn't seem to bother him.

In fact, no one I was with at the time was bothered about my identity, or where I came from. I was just another drifter working my way across the North American conti-nent. This was the beginning of the 1970s and the US had put a man on the moon; but they still hadn't figured out what to do about Vietnam. Ronnie was a misguided young man from a middle-class fam-ily who wanted to be a hippy but still liked to live in the comfort of his parents' home.

I was staying with a couple of guys I'd met on my travels. Billy and Bugsy were part of the hippie counter-culture that sprang up in the late sixties and early sev-enties in the US. Billy was a handsome guy; medium height, blond hair, blue eyes; very easy to get on with, and popular with the ladies. Bugsy earned his nickname from two prominent front teeth; he was also easy to get on with. Ronnie was one of the many people who vis-ited the house from time to time to play cards or just hang out. Billy and Bugsy counted me as a friend, and they got quite upset about the way Ronnie treated me, with his offensive remarks and threats of violence.

I don't know why I had so much trouble with him, but from the start there was conflict between us. Ronnie got himself into quite a lot of trouble anyway; he had a racist attitude and he didn't mind showing it, throwing verbal abuse at anyone who wasn't white.

The first time we met, I was sitting at the table in Billy and Bugsy's kitchen. Ronnie came into the room and immediately he noticed me – oriental features in a group of white faces.

'Hey, Tokyo Joe!' he shouted across the room. I looked up at him, expecting some cheap jibe. What I got was a sawn-off shotgun, pointing straight at me! The atmosphere in the room changed instantly. Everyone was quiet, their eyes flicking between Ronnie and me.

'I am going to blow your brains out!' said Ronnie, waving the shotgun around, and in the process pointing it at half of the people in the room.

I got up and Ronnie came and stood in front of me, the barrel of the gun wavering in front of my heart. At that moment my life really did flash in front of me. Now I know people say this, and it's a bit of a cliché, but that's what happened. Within a few seconds I saw the events of my life like some speeded-up film. Then I was back in the kitchen facing this gun, still there in front of my chest.

I decided I'd play the hero. I'd had enough of life and I was quite prepared to die at this point, but I hated the idea that he might miss me and hit one of the others.

I grabbed the barrel and pulled it tight against my chest.

'Here,' I said, looking him in the eyes. 'Here's where you want to point it, so you don't go hitting anyone else.'

I glanced around at some of the other people in the room. Still silent, they just watched this incident as it played out in front of them. Some of them were slowly easing themselves away from the range of the gun. The end of the barrel pressed hard against my chest, but I could feel the whole weapon shaking in Ronnie's hand.

'OK,' I said. 'Go on, then – pull the damn trigger!'

He looked at me, and then he looked at the gun, and in that moment we both knew that he didn't have the courage to do it. He didn't have the nerve to follow through what he had started, and I despised him for it. He just stood there, dithering.

I snatched the weapon from him, turned it around and smacked him hard across the face. We all heard the noise as the butt of the gun hit Ronnie's mouth, and then he was whimpering on the floor. I think I broke his jaw in the process.

My actions broke the tension; everyone started moving. Bugsy was furious, and he went off to his room to get his own shotgun. Ronnie lay on the floor, blood flowing from his mouth. People ran around the room – most of them didn't know how to handle the situation. Ronnie had a friend called Dave who was present in the room when all this happened. Dave must have realized that things would get worse for his friend if he stayed in the house, so he hauled Ronnie out of the room and dragged him off to the local hospital to get some treatment.

With Ronnie gone, the tension eased a little. I felt completely calm. I decided that I didn't want to see Ronnie again, and I hoped he would do the sensible thing and stay out of my way, because there would be enmity between us from now on. It was only afterwards that I found out that the gun didn't have a firing-pin; even if he had pulled the trigger, nothing would have happened.

I hoped that was the last I'd see of Ronnie, but I was sadly mistaken. I think I must have hurt his pride as well as his jaw, because a few weeks later he came back, again with his friend Dave.

It was just another quiet afternoon in the house. Some of us had been tripping and I had gone to lie down on my bed for a while. A couple of other guys were also there, just playing cards, and everything was really peaceful. Ronnie and Dave turned up, and it was Dave's turn to play the strong man. He came into the kitchen and looked over at the card players.

'Where's Tokyo Joe?' he asked.

'He's in his room, sleeping,' said Glyn, a Hell's Angel from California who was visiting some friends in Ohio.

Glyn visited the house regularly and he wasn't a man you would want to cross.

Dave went towards the bedroom.

'Where you going, then?' asked Glyn.

'I'm going to kick the crap out of him!' said Dave.

Glyn immediately stood up. He had been there when Ronnie had pulled the shotgun in the kitchen, and he shared our disgust at Ronnie's behaviour. He knew what Billy and Bugsy would think if anything happened to me.

'You're not going to do anything to him,' said Glyn. He lunged forward and grabbed Dave, dragging him across the kitchen. The table jolted across the kitchen floor, and one of the chairs flipped over as they headed towards the bathroom. Glyn dragged Dave in there and smashed his head against the sink. He hit the sink so hard, he ended up breaking it.

Dave crumpled onto the floor. 'Please don't hit me any more!' he said, nursing his bruised head.

'You're going to have to pay for that sink,' said Glyn, going back to his card game. This time it was Ronnie's turn to take Dave to the hospital. I didn't know anything about what had happened until I heard the story from Glyn later.

Ronnie kept away after that for a couple of months; and then he turned up again on Christmas Eve. I was at the house and he came in, asking to speak to me. I didn't trust him but I wanted to hear what he had to say.

'I'm going to midnight mass,' he said. 'I'd like you to come with me so that I can make peace with you.'

I wasn't interested in going to any church service, but Ronnie said there were plenty of women – 'broads', he called them – at church, and so we might be able to pull one while we were there. Reluctantly I agreed to go with him. We had to go in his car to get there, and one of his friends came with us. They were fooling around and behaving like idiots from the moment we drove off.

We had been driving just a few minutes when Ronnie stopped the car. I didn't know what he was up to because there wasn't a church in sight – we were in a residential area. Ronnie got out and went up to one of the letter-boxes; he pulled open the flap and took out some of the mail. He then proceeded to open the envelopes, reading the contents of people's private letters to his friend who was with us in the car; they were laughing and giggling together.

'What do you think you're doing?' I said as he got back in the car.

'What's your problem, Tokyo?' said Ronnie.

'My problem?' I said, 'You have the problem, going into people's mailboxes and opening their private letters!'

Ronnie and his friend just laughed at me. We carried on with our journey; and the letters Ronnie had opened were left scattered across the sidewalk.

Before long we had stopped again, and Ronnie was digging around in another mailbox. This time he found a handwritten envelope. The design showed that it was from someone in the military. He ripped open the letter and started to read out the contents. It was a letter from a serviceman to his wife and kids. This guy was on duty in Vietnam and he was saying how sorry he was that he was missing Christmas and was not able to be with his family. It was a very touching letter.

Ronnie laughed and threw the letter on the ground; then he got back in the car. I was disgusted by his behaviour, and as the car pulled away again I told him what I thought of his actions. By this time I'd had enough of Ronnie and his antics.

'Stop the car,' I said. 'I've had enough. I want to get out!'

'You want to get out, eh, Tokyo?' said Ronnie with a sneer. 'OK, then, you get out!' And with that he hit the accelerator and the car started to speed up. This was typical of Ronnie, of course, but I didn't care. I was going to get out, whatever he did. As the car picked up speed I just opened the door and jumped. I'm guessing we must have been doing 50 miles per hour. I hit the road, tumbled over, and then sat up. My trousers were torn but apart from that I was fine. Up ahead, the car screeched to a halt and then started to reverse back towards me.

'Come on, get back in,' he said. I could hear his friend laughing at me.

'No, you can get lost, Ronnie!' I said. 'Go on, before I hit you. I'm going to walk home. I don't want to see you again.'

And I would certainly have hit him, if I had had the chance. But it was Christmas and I didn't want to hit anyone at Christmas. It just didn't seem like the right thing to do in the festive season.

Again, for a few weeks Ronnie kept out of my way. I was glad not to see him, and I'd have been glad never to meet him again. But then sometime in February he came back. He said that he had come back to apologize and to make it up to me.

'Hey, Tokyo – look, I'm sorry about how things have been between us. I don't want any trouble. Tell you what, why don't I buy you a drink in a bar and we make peace – yes?'

My opinion of Ronnie had not changed – I still despised him. He was lucky that I had only belted him once when he had pointed his shotgun at me. I didn't really want to have a drink with him either, but again I decided to go along with what he had suggested. We got in his car and headed, so I thought, for the bar.

We drove away from town and out onto one of the country roads that snaked off towards the smaller communities clustered around Brunswick. I thought maybe he was taking me to some quiet out-of-town place, but then Ronnie pulled into a lay-by and stopped the car. We were completely alone.

OK, I thought. *This is another one of Ronnie's tricks. What's he going to do this time?*

He got out of the car and so I decided to do the same.

'OK, Tokyo,' he said. I could see that he was nervous. He was trying to act cocky but there was fear in his eyes, just like the time when he pulled the shotgun on me.

'I tell you what,' he said. 'We'll sort this out once and for all. Russian roulette – yes?'

He was shaking as he took a revolver from his pocket and loaded a single bullet. The chambers buzzed as he spun them, and then he handed the gun to me. Clearly he wanted me to go first.

I looked around me. Here we were on a deserted road outside Brunswick, and I had a revolver with one bullet. I realized that I could point it at my head or I could point it at Ronnie. My desire to live was not strong, and my pride would not allow me to show any fear at all to this man. So I put the gun to my head, closed my eyes and pulled the trigger.

Click.

I heard the sound of the hammer against the chamber; and then there was just the sound of the wind in the bushes by the roadside. I was still alive.

I brought the weapon down from my head and smiled at Ronnie.

'OK, Ronnie,' I said, 'now you give me another bullet and I will put it in one of the chambers, and then it will be your turn.'

Ronnie looked at me, and his skin was pale against his brown straggly hair.

'Hey, Tokyo,' he said, forcing a laugh, 'come on – I was only joking. We're not really going to play this game.'

But I had just played this game – he had let me do it – and again, like the coward he was, he couldn't face the consequences of what he had started.

I came up to him, still holding the revolver, and I could see him flinching. So I punched him hard in the stomach, and he bent up double with the pain. I pulled him back up, dragged him to the car, and slammed him against the passenger-side window. I held him there and leaned in close to him so that when I spoke he could feel my breath on his sweaty face.

'You listen to me now,' I said. 'If you mess with me one more time – just once more – I will kill you.' I meant it, and he knew it.

I considered taking his car back, but I thought that would be petty, so I just left him shivering and wheezing in the lay-by and started the long walk back to Billy and Bugsy's house.

I never saw Ronnie again, which was a good thing because if he had upset me in any way at all, I would have killed him. Just in time, he learnt his lesson.

Somehow the incident with Ronnie made me restless once more. It had spoilt things for me, even though I was happy in the house. I stayed on with Billy and Bugsy for a while longer, but I was also preparing to move on. I was supposed to be on a tour and I wanted to see other parts of America anyway – particularly California.

When the time seemed right, I collected my stuff, said my goodbyes and headed out towards the freeway so that I could hitch a ride and continue my long journey west across the United States of America.

2

The Hungry Ghosts

Fathers, do not exasperate your children . . .

Ephesians 6:4

I was born in Singapore on 26 March 1949 into a prosperous, upper-middle-class family. Our house had three big bedrooms, we had servants, and there was always food on the table.

My father and mother had an arranged marriage, as was the custom for Buddhist families. The matchmaker arranged for my father and his sister to marry my mother and her brother. I wonder now whether she received double the usual fee for her work.

My parents had seven children – five boys and two girls. I remember my older brother and sister still living with us when I was a small child. My father, in keeping with tradition, had a number of mistresses. We referred to my mother, his wife, as the 'First Wife'. He also had children by one of his mistresses, and we called her the 'Second Mistress'. Any male baby born to the Second Mistress died – an indication within the Buddhist community that a curse was on her. Eventually the family decided to give my youngest brother to her so that she could have a son.

10

My father was a lawyer and my mother was a house-wife, and they started their married life in the aftermath of the Second World War. Singapore was a British Crown Colony up to the time of the Japanese invasion in 1942, and came under British administration again after the war.

I grew up during a time of national upheaval. The people of Singapore had experienced Japanese occupation and British Colonial rule, and they wanted no more of it. When I was 8 years old the island declared unilateral independence, and by the time I was 16 Singapore had joined a federation with Malaysia, and then left to become an independent state. The same government that came to power then is still in power now – the People's Action Party, or PAP. There is no organized opposition, and so the ruling party is the only option for government in Singapore at the moment. What should be a democracy is now starting to look like a dynasty, with the son of the first PAP Prime Minister occupying his father's old office.

While everything was changing for my nation, my brothers and sisters and I continued with our education. My siblings all did well in their careers. My eldest brother became the chairman of the Ministry of Labour and my second eldest brother was an electrician at the Royal Navy base. My oldest sister worked for the Royal Air Force, and my second sister worked at the Nan Yang Technological University.

My father was bald and fat, and looked rather like a Buddha. He would go out gambling and drinking in the evening and would not return home until the early hours; sometimes the drink made him angry when he got home. His behaviour made the atmosphere in the house tense and blighted the first years of life for all of us. He used to bully my mother, and I resented him for it, and I don't think any of my siblings liked him either.

When my father was in a good mood we would talk, and those were the best times I had with him. When I was younger I was a Beatles fan; I had a Beatles hair-cut and Beatles clothes and shoes. I remember one occasion when we were watching them on the television, and my father asked me if I liked the music. I said I did, so he gave me some money to buy some Beatles boots and records. He must have been in an exceptionally good mood that day.

Sometimes he would come home with some Chinese takeaway and would wake me up so that I could eat it with him – this would be about one or two in the morning. I was always nervous when he did this because he would also be drunk, and if anything went wrong he would fly into a temper. One time he sent me out to buy some Chinese food and I didn't pay attention at the shop and the chef put chilli sauce in with the food. Now my father never liked chilli sauce, and when he discovered what had happened he was very angry and made me eat the whole lot.

By contrast, my mother was a very calm person. She had a petite figure and she was in her nineties when she died. She was always very caring and very sacrificial in her dealings with us. Even though, like my father, she beat me, I know that she did love me. She was a very strict Buddhist, which meant that she was a vegetarian, she prayed a lot, and she would not knowingly kill any creature, even an ant. She would often go to the temple to pray and she tried to help those around her, and when grandchildren came along she did all she could to help out. We had my oldest brother's son staying with us for a few years after he was born. He was about 5 years old when he went back to his parents. My oldest brother's daughter,

Catherine, came and stayed with us until she was about 8 or 9; my mother loved having her around.

We grew up in an atmosphere of comfortable prosperity, even while Singaporean society was going through upheaval and the country moved from being a colony to independent statehood.

I can recall the Singaporeans rioting against the British in the 1950s; at the time we were a nation hungry for independence. By the 1960s the British had gone and the riots, when they happened, were between the Malay and Chinese people. What happened in Malaysia tended to influence events on the Island of Singapore. The Singaporean Chinese would hear stories about Chinese people in Malaysia being beaten up or killed, and they responded by rioting with the Singaporean Malays.

But these were sporadic incidents. On the whole people lived together in harmony, and the ethnic tension did not spill over into large-scale violence. In primary school we played a game where we threw a tennis ball at one another. Whoever had the ball could throw it at anyone, but everyone else would jump on whoever had the ball and beat them up. We played this game before and after school, and often the boisterous play would turn into violence. Usually the teams divided by race; so the Chinese would take on the Malays, with the Indians and the Eurasians also classified as Malay for the purposes of the game.

Even within the majority Chinese population, there were tensions. The English-educated Chinese, like me, did not like the Chinese-educated Chinese; we thought of them all as communists.

As well as the racial tensions, Singaporean society as a whole was very superstitious. A variety of cultures and faiths existed on the Island, and so we were never far from a holiday or festival of one kind or another.

The highlight of the year was the Hungry Ghost Festival. The seventh month of the Chinese calendar is traditionally known as the Ghost Month. In that month the spirits of the dead are said to rise from the lower realm for a 'holiday' on the earth and also to visit their families. The festival, held on the fifteenth day of the month, was the climax of a series of celebrations, including Chinese opera, acted out on the streets. The performers started up at about 11 o'clock in the morning and they would go on till about 4 o'clock. Then they would have a break and start again at about 7 o'clock and end at about 11.

We would set up an altar and start praying to the hungry ghosts, asking them not to torment us; we would even leave food out for them. There would be pigs, chickens and ducks roasted in the street. We offered prayers for our ancestors and burnt incense, whilst local shops and street-vendors organized and paid for the festival and the street-fairs.

For our part, my siblings and I released little paper boats onto the water of our local lake, supposedly to give the ghosts direction on their travels. We burnt paper replicas of possessions that the ghosts might need in the afterlife – things like TVs, radios and cars. There were no electronic games in those days, of course, so we played with tops and marbles and kites. We also made bullets from cigarette boxes, shooting these at each other with rubber bands.

We celebrated not one but four New Years – the Chinese New Year, the Malay New Year, the Indian New Year, and the English New Year. Then there were other festivals and holidays – Divali, Ramadan, Buddha's birthday, and more.

At the Spring Festival people would visit the graves of their ancestors to clean them, cut the grass, and offer flowers. Everyone took food and there would be a picnic afterwards; leftovers were taken home for a party.

Then there was the Dragon Boat Festival, which had its roots in a popular myth. The story went like this:

Once upon a time there was a very good, wise man, and he lived in a town by a river. A very bad dragon lived in the river and the townsfolk would sacrifice their own people to the dragon to appease it. But the wise man said:

'We should not sacrifice people to the dragon. This is a bad thing to do!'

But the people did not believe him.

'I tell you what,' said the wise man. 'Make a triangular cake and put rice in it, and feed that to the dragon. He will eat too much and die.'

So the people did this. They made the cakes and threw them to the dragon, and he ate them all. In fact he ate too much and died. The people were happy because they no longer needed to give any of their number as a sacrifice to the dragon. So every year on the fifth day of the fifth month, people marked the event by making and eating triangular cakes with rice and meat in them.

Also on that day the Chinese celebrated the Festival of the Couple. Again, this festival was rooted in popular myth.

The story was that the gods would occasionally visit the earth and see what the mortals were doing. On one such visit a poor farmer saw one of the goddesses and, entranced by her beauty, he captured her. They had two children together, but the goddess was herself the daughter of the mighty heavenly King, and he was not happy with this. So he sent the heavenly warriors down to kidnap her and bring her back, even though she had fallen in love with the farmer.

The farmer could not go and get her back because there was a river between him and the gods in heaven.

So in his anguish the man began to cry out, telling of his sorrow at the loss of his lover. Eventually one of the heavenly King's counsellors, a wise and learned sage, heard this and stepped in to make a deal.

The heavenly King said the farmer and the goddess could meet once a year, and so the sage asked the birds of the air to form a bridge across the river. The birds did this and the lovers were able to meet on the bridge, once a year as the heavenly King had decreed.

On the fifteenth day of the eighth month there was the Moon Cake Festival. These 'moon cakes' were in fact sweet lotus-seed cakes. Children would come out at night with lanterns and parade in the streets. This festival was used as a way of communicating revolution during the Ching Dynasty. China is a big place, and usually on this festival people sent their friends moon cake. The Red Flower Society, a triad gang of the Hun people, decided to have a revolution. They got the people to put a date – the fifteenth day of the eighth month – on some paper and hide the paper in the sweet cakes, and pass them round. So the Hun people all learnt of the date of the revolution and rose up on that day against the Ching people, and that was the end of the Ching Dynasty.

In the ninth month there was a birthday festival for the Nine Dukes (Kou Wong Yea). The people carried big incense-burners and statues of the deities were paraded in the streets using palanquins.

On 9 September we also celebrated Singapore Independence Day, a time when myth and superstition were replaced by nationalist fervour.

Not all our time was taken up with festivals, of course. We loved to go fishing as well. We would dig worms out of the ground and use them for bait; sometimes we would use bread or tapioca as well.

These were the happier aspects of my childhood – playing with my siblings and friends, and enjoying the vibrant life of a community that knew how to celebrate. The biggest problem for me, as it was for many of the children in Singapore, was the oppressive discipline that we all suffered at that time. Not only did I have a drunken and unreliable father; I also suffered under the strict regime applied in our school.

Corporal punishment was an accepted part of school life. We were caned regularly, and sometimes the teacher hit my knuckles with a ruler. At home my brothers and sisters and I were regularly caned. Also, because my youngest brother had been given to the Second Mistress, I became the youngest boy; so my older siblings bullied me as well.

I had a very good friend at primary school called Alan Chow; I would go to his house and play. He had an orchard behind his house and we would go and get fruit from the trees. He lived near a Pentecostal church called Bethel Church. It had an American pastor – an old guy with grey hair. In keeping with the Pentecostal tradition, he never wore a dog-collar, just a smart suit and tie. He always looked friendly and wise to me.

Alan started to go there when he heard that they were giving out pencils with Mickey Mouse and Donald Duck erasers on them. They told Alan that if he could bring his friend along he would get a bookmark, and his friend would get a pencil with a Mickey Mouse eraser. Alan wanted a bookmark and saw me as a way to get one.

'Come to church with me,' he said one day.

'I can't come to church,' I said. 'I'm a Buddhist.'

'If you don't come to the church with me,' replied Alan, 'then you can't come and play in the orchard.'

Now I loved playing in the orchard, running between the trees and collecting the fruit, so I decided to go. I went to the Sunday school and I got my pencil with the Mickey Mouse eraser, and I presume Alan got his bookmark. A few weeks later they said I would get a bookmark if I brought a friend along. So I took one of my neighbour's kids to church; he got his pencil and I got my bookmark, but then he didn't come back after that.

My mother did not object to me going to church – she thought that there were many gods and having one more was fine. I don't think my father was bothered one way or another by the issue at all.

My interest in the Sunday school was just beginning to wane when the leadership of the church came up with a new scheme. If I were able to come along for ten consecutive weeks I would get a Bible! I was determined to meet this challenge. I missed one or two weeks and had to start again, but eventually I did go for ten consecutive weeks. I think I enjoyed the achievement of overcoming a challenge more than the actual fact of receiving my reward.

Then I went on a twenty-six-week course with the church called 'Gateway through life'. I worked my way through this course, and at the end they gave me an embossed certificate. By this time simply coming to church was quite fun; some of the youth leaders played modern music; the pastor wasn't too happy about that, but us younger folks loved it. The church leaders were pretty strict; they told us that we should not go to movies, especially films that involved cowboys and Indians or Superman; we were not to watch TV, and we were not to read war comics. Church became another place with rules and restrictions, something else to rebel against.

Despite some tensions with the youth, things went well for the church until the pastor went on a year's sabbatical and in his absence a young couple came in and took over. They were not like the pastor; they dressed smartly like him but they had a rather superior attitude and did not seem to project the sense of paternal care that he had. While we were struggling with their approach to things, more problems occurred.

Some of the congregation felt that the wife of the couple was not behaving as she should. This caused trouble in the church and made me very angry. I began to wonder whether Christians had a habit of not practising what they preached. Eventually I left and decided to have nothing more to do with church. I never left Buddhism, but any Christian influence that might have moderated my behaviour was now gone.

In my anger with the church I became rather like Paul before his 'Road to Damascus' conversion. I persecuted anyone of my age who was a Christian. I remember in secondary school there were two teachers, Mr Pang and Mr Lee, and they were Christians. They used to take students to church on a Friday and I used to persecute these fellow students of mine.

I would spit on the Bible in front of them, tear up their tracts, and threaten them with violence. All of this came out of my anger with Christians who, in my view, had double standards.

I began to think of the Christian faith as a white man's religion. I remember hearing someone talking about Christianity. They said: 'They bring you the Bible, and while you are looking at the Bible you are distracted, and the next thing you know, your land disappears from beneath your feet and becomes part of the great British Empire!'

I was in a mood to take all this to heart. It fuelled my anger, and pretty soon I thought all whites were Christians, and I hated all of them.

Meanwhile I was progressing through school. I moved from primary school to the Serangoon Secondary

School, where I studied Maths, Geography, History, Art, Algebra, Geometry, Biology, Chemistry and English. I had some business skills, and I enjoyed doing deals – buying and selling things. Not everything I did was honest business. I had a very nasty temper and I found that people looked to me for leadership. If bargaining didn't work, I would sometimes resort to intimidation. I organized some youth gangs and practised extortion on my fellow students, telling them that they had to buy cigarettes for me. The terrified students would buy me cigarettes and I would smoke them or sell them on.

Sometimes a number of us would go and fight with students from other schools. I think I was about 15 or 16 years old at this time. Incredibly, I was still going to the Sunday school at the church whilst all this was going on; and I did not see any contradiction between the very different activities in my life.

As I approached the end of my time in education, the pattern of business and violence was set. I would beat people up, I would take kites from other kids – and I would make business deals with people, or force deals on them.

Some of my cousins were gangsters involved in pornography, prostitution and extortion. One of my cousins ended up in jail on Sentosa Island. There was a riot at the prison while he was there and the governor was murdered. The authorities hanged him for his part in that insurrection.

The company I kept helped to shape the person I became. Some of the people I associated with had a nasty streak to them, but because I was their leader, I felt that I had to be more nasty and violent than them, to set an example. Some of them had older brothers who were gangsters.

I took my anger and pride into adult life. I was a leader, but I felt that I could only lead by example, and that example was a hard attitude backed up with occasional violence. I nurtured the anger that I felt; I knew it spurred me on to do the things I wanted to do.

As my school days drew to a close, I was impatient to grow up and become independent. My father and my eldest brother had told me that when I was old enough to make my own money I could do whatever I wanted to, and I was determined to take them at their word. I wanted to escape, to get out from the oppressive environments of home and school, and live how I wanted to live instead of being under someone else's rules. Rather like one of the Hungry Ghosts, I wanted to escape from the hell that had restrained me for so long and to roam free from the oppression I had suffered.

My chance came in 1967 when I turned 18. At last I was able to leave school and get a job. I had been waiting for this moment and now that it had arrived, I was going to take full advantage of it.

3

The World of Work

Teachers open the door. You enter by yourself.

Chinese proverb

I got a job at the Singapore Life Insurance Company, working as a sales manager. I was only 18 but I already knew how to buy and sell, how to do business. In fact I knew two ways to do business – the nice way and the nasty way.

I was a confident young man, but I knew that I had a lot to learn. Fresh out of school, I turned to another set of teachers to help me. One of the people I learnt from in those early days was a man called George Leiu. George was like a mentor to me; I listened to what he said, and I observed his actions because I knew I could learn from him.

When I arrived at the company, George joined my sales team. He must have been about 50 years old and he was a sophisticated and handsome man. He looked rather like Sean Connery, and I was very impressed by his style. At around five feet eight, he was taller than many of his colleagues and he was always immaculately dressed. He spoke with a kind of natural charm and he had presence about him, a charisma that helped him in his social life and in his work. George told me he was a Freemason, although at the time I did not know what that meant. He offered to get me into the 'club'. Occasionally, he would share some little piece of wisdom with me.

'In any situation,' he would say to me, 'try to observe and learn. Don't look like you're very smart. If people think you're cleverer than them, they won't teach you anything.'

George was quite a private person. He would only speak when required; his address was a secret, and I could only contact him through his girlfriend, who worked at one of the daily newspapers.

Soon after I started, the company introduced a new weekly Life Insurance Policy. Customers could buy the policy in units, and the cost was $1.50 per unit per week. The sum assured was $1,000 per unit and customers had to pay into the policy for fourteen weeks before they could make a claim. George sold a lot of these policies, and was confident that he could sell many more. He came to see me in the office one day with a proposal:

'Hi, Bobby,' he said. ('Bobby' was my Anglicized name and I tended to use it with everyone I met in business.)

'Hello, George. How's business?'

'Very good,' said George with a flourish, 'but it could be even better!'

'Could it? How?' I asked him.

'With these new policies,' said George, smiling. 'I have made good money selling them here in Singapore, but I could make even better money selling them elsewhere.'

'Where would you go to sell them then?' I asked, intrigued.

'I have connections with some lumberjacks out in Borneo,' said George. 'I could sell the policies to those guys if I was allowed to go out there for a couple of weeks.'

I was happy to let George go off and do business wherever he could. He took one of our receipt books away with him, travelled to Borneo, and a week or so later he came back with a lot of business. He had made the company a great deal of money.

A few months later, George came to me once more. He wanted to go out to Borneo again and sell more of the policies there. He told me that he wanted four receipt books this time, so confident was he about the amount of business he would get. Because he had been so successful on his last trip, I was happy to let him go with all the receipt books he wanted.

George went off, but a few weeks later I got a call from him to say that he had lost the receipt books on his travels. Without the receipt books we would not be able to record who had paid what for their policies. We advertised in the newspapers to try to get the books back, but we never recovered them. This was quite an embarrassment for the company, and pretty soon after that George resigned.

Time passed and I began to forget about him; I just got on with business. Then one day I got a phone call at the office, and it was George, inviting me to lunch. He wanted to meet at some quiet place away from the office, and I agreed to go out there to meet him. When we met he was quite agitated, looking around at the other customers; there was none of his old confident charm.

'I have to leave the country!' he told me over our meal. 'If you need to contact me you will have to do it through my girlfriend.'

I didn't ask him too many questions at the time, but later I discovered that George was a con man, and a very clever and ambitious one at that. It transpired that he had conned a Japanese bank and a Borneo timber company out of $20 million. To the timber company he had been posing as an agent for the bank, and to the bank he had been posing as an agent for the timber company. He had managed to defraud both parties in the process.

With sums like this involved, George knew that there would be a contract out on his life. The Indonesians were after him and so where the Japanese. I was rather flattered to discover that I was the only one whom he trusted; and he had risked his life even to have lunch with me. I was also the only one who knew about the link to him through his girlfriend. He sent me a letter, via her, about a year after he disappeared. I didn't tell the police I had received the letter although, of course, they were after him as well.

The last I heard of George (again via his girlfriend) was that he had joined a travelling circus. How much truth there was in it, I don't know. He was very fit, so it was entirely possible that he had done this, although why a man with $20 million would need to join a travelling circus is a question that I was never able to ask him.

After this I realized that he must have sold the receipt books somewhere. He had probably collected hundreds of premium instalments and given out receipts that were now worthless. In the end there was no insurance for these people, so he had the workers as well as the management after him. Crooked though he was, I loved George; he taught me about life and business. I always remembered his advice about not showing how clever I was, and that I should not expect my environment to adapt itself to me – rather, I should adapt myself to my environment.

In time, I began to mix with more people in the insurance company. Most of them were honest, decent people who just wanted to make a living. We would go out drinking at local bars and pick up the 'hostesses' who worked there. These girls were essentially prostitutes and they received protection from the gangs in exchange for a cut of their earnings.

Spirits were popular as a drink at this time. We drank cognac, whisky, brandy, rum and gin. It was rare to drink beer – maybe someone might have a couple of beers in the hot weather.

As well as socializing with my colleagues, I was mixing with a number of gangsters. Some were illiterate, whilst others were very well educated. The gangster class spanned the racial divide, with Chinese, Malays and Indians represented. The gangs made their money from prostitution, extortion, blue movies and protection. There was some drugs activity in those days, but not much. In Singapore each gang had a number rather than a name: 14k, 18, 24, 36, 08, 808, 329 and 969. I belonged to the 329 gang, and our speciality was showing illegal blue movies. I got involved in gang fights, I collected protection money, I made deals, and I visited people who hadn't paid back loans. I did all this whilst holding down a job at the insurance company.

I worked for the insurance company for about nine months before I decided to change jobs and move to a travel agency. In fact, I decided to work for three different travel agencies, all at the same time. I would go to one office at 9 a.m., to another office at 9.30 and to yet another at 10 – I pretended to be at all of these offices all the time, and I was on the payroll for all three companies. I also supplemented my income by selling on business from one agency to another. So if someone bought a plane ticket, I would pass the business from one company to another and then to another, so that I got the commission from all three companies. In the middle of all this, I still found time to sell some insurance. I had a lot of money coming in, and I was very busy; the problem was that through gambling I always ended up losing more than I earned. For all my efforts to earn income, I still ended up in debt.

I enjoyed gambling; it was my passion and my weakness. I would bet on the horses, I would play mah-jong and card games; there were a variety of gambling activities, but all of them involved me losing money.

At least I had acquired the independence that I wanted. I was only 18 and I was still living at home. I had my own keys and my parents never told me when to be back; I was earning my own money now and I could do what I liked. My mother was usually asleep when I got home at night, and my father was usually still out. By now I had grown out of being afraid of my father. He was out seeing women and so was I; he was out drinking and so was I.

There was also a more sinister side to my life by this time. My involvement with the gangs had introduced me to the occult and black magic.

There were rogue Buddhist monks from Thailand who had brought some occult practices to Singapore. Black magic was taken very seriously by the gangs, and each gang would have its own shaman. The shaman would make a potion for the gang members to drink before they went out – it stopped us from feeling pain when we were in a fight.

Perhaps even more sinister were the 'little devils' that we reared. When a child died, the shaman would put a piece of wood in the ground above the grave, without the family's knowledge, and this was supposed to 'steal' the soul of the child. They carved the wood into a little figure and put it in a bottle. The shaman would chant over the piece of wood and give it to one of the gangsters. We had to 'feed' our devils periodically with a few grains of rice; over time my devil grew and I had to transfer it to a bigger bottle. If you had one of these little devils, you could ask it to do things for you; for example, you could ask it to tell you which horse was going to win a race. It didn't always work, of course. One day I went racing with my little devil and it lost me a lot of money, so I threw it away in disgust.

On other occasions the shaman wrote incantations on yellow paper; we rolled these papers up and put them in a *tanga* – a sealed bronze tube, the size of a 1-inch nail but three times thicker. I wore mine in my belt. A *tanga* was supposed to give protection, but if your opponent dipped his knife in pure black dog-blood, he could then chop you, even if you were wearing a *tanga*. With all the gangs using black magic, these occult activities became something that bound us rather than conferring advantage.

Sometimes we asked the shaman to do something that would charm women into liking us. If you approached a shaman for this service, they would pray over a needle and stick it in you, and the woman you wanted would find you attractive. You could also try to make someone insane. These occult activities are still practised today in some South-East Asian countries.

I was involved in many fights, but the worst thing that happened to me was losing some teeth when I was punched. It was a miracle that I came away from these gang fights relatively unscathed. The gangs would fight openly, with machetes and knives. There were fights in bars; sometimes people would fight over the hostesses, and sometimes they would throw bottles at each other. These fights would often spill over and affect other people in the bar.

On one occasion there was a big gang fight during the Hungry Ghost Festival. Everyone was celebrating and the gangs joined in. Our gang had organized a banquet on the third day of the festivities. We were in the middle of our banquet when one of the rival gangs turned up and started causing trouble for us. We could not allow this to happen without some response, so we had to settle the matter with a machete fight.

These gang fights could be vicious, and I knew people who died as a result of their injuries – such as Anthony, who was in my gang in Singapore, and Billy, who was in a gang in Chinatown in London.

Now that I had a job, and did whatever I wanted, my relationship with my father deteriorated still further. Sometimes my mother would have to act as a go-between for the two of us, but the relationship had really broken down by this time.

I remember one occasion when my father had beaten up my mother. I had been out, and when I got home I discovered her, beaten and bruised. I was so angry that the next night I went out and found him and told him that if he came home that evening, I would kill him. I spent that evening sharpening my machete.

I realised that things could not go on like this, so I decided to leave home. I quietly applied for a passport and started to make preparations for leaving. The fact that I worked for travel agencies made it easy for me to book all of the tickets I needed. It took me about three months to organize everything, but eventually I had my passport and my tickets and I was ready to go.

I wanted to travel and see the world, and I also wanted to have a fresh start in my life. Leaving home would give me a chance to do both of these things.

4

A European Tour

Follow the local custom when you go to a foreign place.

Chinese proverb

There were other reasons for me to leave home, not just the deteriorating relationship with my father. I was having an affair with a married woman at this time, and had been planning to go to Australia with her. We had talked about it and started to make arrangements, and then out of the blue, she decided to go back to her husband. I took it badly and was very upset, but I had to accept the situation.

I had also run up a lot of gambling debts. Gambling is part of the culture in Singapore, especially for gangsters, and I owed a lot of people a lot of money. Some of them wouldn't be too fussy about how they got it back, and I began to fear for my life. I realized that I needed to go on my own, and I'd be going for good. I had booked a round-the-world ticket through the various travel agencies where I worked, and of course I had claimed the commission – three times over.

I decided to start in Thailand, so that I could visit the gangsters I knew there. I hoped to be able to make some easy money while I was there. On the morning I was due to go, I went to see my father. I made sure my mother wasn't around when I spoke to him.

'I've come to tell you that I am leaving,' I said. 'I'm not coming back here.'

He looked me in the eyes and said, 'Son, if you walk out of that door on two legs you will walk back in on four legs within a month!'

He meant that if I walked out now, within a month I would be crawling back like a dog begging for mercy. My answer to him was simple:

'I'm not going to come back here until you are dead.'

That was the last time I ever spoke to my father. I never saw him again, and I didn't see my mother again until she visited London in 1976, some seven years later.

I told her that I was going on holiday to Japan and that I would be back in a couple of weeks. I also told my sister that I was going to Japan, and I asked her to give me a lift to the airport. I didn't talk to my brothers about it because they had all left home by then.

I secured a window seat on the plane and as we took off I looked out and watched Singapore disappear behind me. I saw my home, the streets I knew – my whole life up to that point – shrinking away from me. There were tears in my eyes as the plane gained altitude and I watched it all fade behind the clouds. I would not be crying again for a long, long time.

We landed in Thailand, and I went to see some of my associates there with a view to getting some work. I went out drinking with a few of these guys, and found myself relaxing for the first time in years. The desire to work and earn money slipped away, so that my time in Thailand turned out to be the holiday that I had told everyone I was having. I stayed with some friends and had a good time, drinking and gambling and womanizing. It was a cheap way to have a holiday. Sometimes we

would go out into the country and do some target practice with guns. We shot up bottles and cans, whatever
we could find, and then it was back to the bars in the city
for a good night out.

I stayed in Thailand for just under two months, and
then I decided to move on and travel to the other side of
the world. My next stop was going to be Denmark. I
would stay there just one night before moving on to the
place I really wanted to visit – Sweden. I said goodbye to
my associates and boarded the long-haul flight for
Europe.

The plane touched down in Denmark in the morning
and I checked into the hotel. Although I was only staying for one day, I was determined to make the most of
my time there. That meant clubs and bars, drinking and
women.

That evening I went to a place called the Maxim Club,
and I picked up a girl. She was just a prostitute but she
had blonde hair, blue eyes and a lovely figure. I wanted
to have sex with her, but first we decided to have a drink.
We stayed in the club, and she drank Scandinavian
schnapps. I ordered her a double, and then another, and
then another. She was drinking so much that in the end I
just bought a whole bottle of this stuff for her. We got
drunk together, and by the early hours of the morning I
had given up all hope of taking this woman to bed with
me; instead I decided to buy her some breakfast.

We went to a café and ordered some food and coffee.
By now it was about seven in the morning, but she still
wanted to drink! She even asked for some schnapps for
her coffee; I told her I wasn't buying that, just breakfast.
Also I was beginning to think about when I would need
to get to the airport for my flight.

At the next table there were a couple of Norwegian
sailors. They were pretty big, hard-looking guys and

soon she started to speak to them in her own language. I couldn't understand a word she was saying, and after spending all that money on her, I wasn't happy about being cut out by a couple of 'locals'. The sailors could sense my anger and they started to look at me in an aggressive way. I guessed they must have thought I was just some arrogant foreigner. Whatever they thought, I wasn't going to sit there like an idiot while these three spoke to each other in a language I didn't understand.

'Hey guys,' I said in English, 'I'm buying this girl breakfast, OK? But no more alcohol; she's been drinking all night, OK?'

They stared at me, and it was clear that they had no idea what I was talking about.

'Look here,' I said, 'if you two want to be suckers, that's fine by me, but I'm not going to be a sucker for anyone. Do you want to be suckers, yes?' I nodded and smiled at them.

'*Jah, jah!*' they said; but then it must have dawned on them that I was making fun of them, so that made them even more angry.

The girl watched this exchange through a drunken haze whilst I carried on talking to the Norwegians.

'I've spent nearly $500 on this girl,' I said. 'If you want to pay for some of that, you're welcome. Listen, I don't even want you to be a full sucker. You can pay me $250 and be a half sucker, OK?'

They could see that I was continuing to make fun of them, and I knew they would want to do something about it. I was comfortable with this sort of situation, where aggression can turn to violence. I called over the waiter and ordered some more boiling-hot water to have with my breakfast, and then I unscrewed the top of the pepper-pot that was on the table. The water arrived just as the Norwegians were getting up from their table; I could see they were heading in my direction. I watched them both as they approached, and prepared myself for a fight.

As they came to edge of the table I stood up, took the pepper in one hand and the hot water in the other, and threw the whole lot at them. They both screamed, so I followed this up by smacking them, and the woman, with the water jug.

There was uproar in the café. The woman screamed, and the sailors shouted; customers turned round to see what was going on; and the owners started to come towards us. We must have made an interesting sight: a Chinaman clutching a steaming water-jug, some growling Norwegians, and a rather drunk prostitute nursing her head.

Clearly it was time to leave. I put the jug down and walked briskly to the door. Outside I found a taxi rank and got a lift back to my hotel. I needed to leave anyway if I was going to make my flight. At the hotel I grabbed my things, paid my bill, and hurried off to the airport. I was just in time to check in.

I had met someone in Thailand who had a business contact in Sweden, so I was hoping to follow up this connection. But my main reason for going to Sweden was to catch up with an old pen pal who I used to write to when I was at school; I had lost touch with her for four or five years. Her name was Eva and she lived near Uppsala. I didn't even tell her I was coming, but she had invited me over some time ago, and I considered the invitation to be still open. My plan was to marry her and start a new life with her.

At the airport I phoned my business contact, Mr Chen, and arranged to meet him for dinner. I asked him if he would order the national dish for me, and he was happy to oblige.

When we met for dinner he duly ordered the national dish, and when it arrived I saw that it consisted of raw herring in a kind of vinegar mixture. It tasted so bad that I felt sick, so I exchanged it for his plate of shrimps.

Then we talked business. Mr Chen's mother ran the operation, and I began to think about how I could make money out of this opportunity. First of all, because the mother was away for two months, I was able to stay with Mr Chen, and we lived like a couple of bachelors – always out at parties.

After I had enjoyed myself for a while I decided to phone my pen pal. I told her I was in Sweden and was coming to stay with her.

'How long are you going to stay?' she asked.

'For as long as I can!' I told her.

'I must ask my husband,' she replied.

She's married! I thought. This was very unwelcome news.

'Your husband?' I asked, rather stupidly.

'Yes, I'm married. Maybe you can come and visit for the weekend.'

Well, of course, I wasn't interested in her after that. I decided to forget all about her, and because my main reason for staying in Sweden had disappeared, I decided to move on to Holland.

I was able to get a flight to Amsterdam, but by now my funds were running out. I needed to earn some money, so I went to the Rotterdam docks to find a job as a sailor or dock labourer.

Seeing the reality of what was required of a merchant navy sailor made me think again about what I wanted to do. It was hard, unpleasant work, with unsociable hours; definitely not like my usual line of trade.

I got in touch with some people I used to know in Singapore who had moved to Amsterdam some years earlier. I told them I was looking for work, and so I ended up helping out in the Chinese gambling den in Amsterdam and also in a restaurant there. I earned a bit of cash as a bouncer. This was the kind of work I was used to – much better than working as a sailor!

As I settled down to life in Holland, I realized that whilst I was content with my work, I was not really happy. In fact I had never really been happy and I knew something was missing in my life, although I did not know what it was. I thought maybe I needed to find a woman and settle down. As I grew more restless, I decided to deal with the situation in the only way I knew how – to move on to somewhere new. I thought about where I should go to next and decided on a trip to England. At least everyone there spoke English – a language I was familiar with.

I bought my ticket, packed my bag and headed for the airport. I knew people in London, and as soon as I was off the plane I went to visit them. I made the acquaintance of one guy, who introduced himself to me as Tony, and he told me how we could make some money. He had dark brown hair and dark eyes, and he had the basic requirements of a con man: he was both charming and unscrupulous.

We went to visit a lady that he knew. Her boyfriend was in Singapore, so I told her I was her boyfriend's sister's fiancé, and I was in England to study and I had lost my luggage. I asked her if I could borrow £500 – a lot of money in 1970.

She bought my story, and borrowed the money from her boss. Clutching the £500, my friend and I went off to a bookie in Kensington and we put all the money on a horse. I can still remember its name – Raffingora, and it was ridden by Lester Piggott. The horse won, coming in at 5–2. There was no tax in those days, so I walked away with £1,750. I felt like I owned the world! I had been off the plane for just 24 hours and already I had nearly £2,000 in my pocket.

The lucky streak that I imagined I was having continued. I went straight down to the Chinese casino in London with Tony and managed to make another few thousand pounds. I didn't return the £500 to the girl. I never intended to – I don't think that would have crossed my mind.

In the casino, as in any Chinese casino, we played *Pai Gow*, a kind of dominoes game. Each person in the round has four dominoes; everyone plays against the banker and bets on the results.

My lucky streak did not last, and in the next few days I lost all the money as I carried on gambling. I knew that I had to get a job, so I made some enquiries and ended up working for a Mr Ling at the Cathay Restaurant in Victoria.

I stayed at Mr Ling's house while I was in London. I had a room, but I had to provide my own food. I didn't even get a key to the house; that meant that on a Sunday evening I'd have to be back by 10 p.m. because they would have to let me in. Mr Ling and his family were Christians and on Sunday mornings the house was quiet because they all went to church.

Unfortunately, Mr Ling's behaviour confirmed my low opinion of Christians because while I was working for him he swindled me. At the restaurant the English customers gave tips to all the waiters and we handed these in to Mr Ling, who recorded all the amounts in a notebook. This did not worry me because I thought he would share the money out amongst the staff at some point. The end of the week came and we got nothing. Then the end of the month came and still we got nothing. This really bothered me, so I went to talk to him about it.

'Mr Ling,' I said, 'what's happened to all the tips?'

'The tips belong to me,' he said. We never discussed the matter again, but I began to think about how I could swindle him back. I bided my time, and then one day I approached him.

'Mr Ling, I am hoping to go to university in the New Year and I need to open a bank account. Can you take me to open an account?'

'Sure,' he said, and so he took me to the bank and introduced me to the manager there. He told the manager that I was his nephew. I opened an account and paid in some gambling winnings that I had accrued.

I was paid £8 a week, but he increased this to £10 while he went home to Singapore to see his sick mother. While he was away I was the head waiter. He was still cheating me even while he was in Singapore, because he got his daughter and nephew to record and keep the tips. I became quite rude with some of the customers so that they would not give me a tip, and I told my best customers not to leave tips for me. I didn't try to pocket the tips myself – I saw that as petty. I was always after the big amounts – and anyway, I had a plan in mind to get my own back on Mr Ling.

In all Mr Ling was away for three months. When he came back I continued to work for him and I continued to let him cheat me. At the same time I started to accumulate cheque-books for my account. In those days you could keep asking for cheque-books, and the bank never looked at how many cheques you had used. I accumulated about eight of them and there were about thirty pages in each book – 240 cheques in all. I was beginning to prepare for my departure.

I went to a travel agent and booked myself a ticket to America. At the end of that week I also changed a cheque with my boss for £1,000. I knew it was going to bounce, but that simply meant that I had settled my financial affairs with him.

On the Friday and Saturday of that week I visited as many banks and exchanges in London as I could and I cashed cheques at each one. At the time you could cash as many cheques as you wanted in any one day. I took the money and added it to the £1,000 I had already received from Mr Ling. This man was supposed to be a Christian and an elder in his church, but as far as I was concerned he was a hypocrite. I felt no guilt about taking his money, or money from the banks. Armed with a plane ticket and a lot of dollars, I headed to the airport for my flight to the USA.

5

The Big Apple

Never seek illicit wealth.

Confucius, The Book of Rites (Liji)

My first stop was New York. I followed my usual routine and checked into one of the better hotels. I always did this if I didn't have a contact in town; I figured that if you spent enough time in the bar of an expensive hotel, sooner or later you would meet someone who was either a useful contact or ripe for a con.

I ended up at the Piccadilly Hotel in Times Square. I checked in and headed down to the bar, where I soon made the acquaintance of a Chinese lad by the name of Me Yee who worked there. I stayed in the hotel and visited the bar and drank a lot; and the more I drank, the more I became friends with Mr Yee. He was certainly good company for me during my first days in the Big Apple. At five feet nine and with a well-built physique, he was both tall and big for a Chinese. He had a cheerful disposition and seemed like a decent kind of guy.

As the days passed, Mr Yee and I became best pals; but my hotel bill was beginning to mount up. He knew that I was short of cash and so he offered me a place to stay at his grandfather's antique shop in Times Square. I was very happy to get out of the expensive hotel and into more affordable accommodation.

The shop was an amazing place – an Aladdin's cave of Chinese antiques and novelties. The sales area was just a small part of the whole store, like the visible tip of a giant iceberg. Behind the shop floor were store-rooms full of antiquities, as well as formal living quarters and little areas where someone might be able to make a bed and sleep. I found a corner in one of the store-rooms and made this place my home for the rest of my time in New York.

Mr Yee was now my house-mate, and he took me to the Chinese casino in New York. He had some connection with the Tongs, a Chinese gangster organization in the city, and he managed to get me a job with them as a bouncer and croupier at the casino.

With the antique shop as a base, I started to explore the city a little. In New York, China Town is next to Little Italy, and so I began to eat in the Italian restaurants, making the acquaintance of a number of the Mafia people there.

One guy I got to know really well there was an Italian-American called Mario. Like me, he would sometimes eat at one of the restaurants in the Italian quarter. He had connections with the Families and with the Tongs. We never did business together but we were friends and I enjoyed his company. Our paths were destined to cross again in the future, and through Mario I would be able to give a young couple the holiday of a lifetime.

* * * *

I enjoyed working as a croupier and bouncer; but unfortunately, the casinos were my weakness and I soon started gambling again and losing money, just as I had in

Singapore and London. As the debts mounted up, I started looking for more opportunities to make money, and eventually I got a job at the docks, carrying in fish from the boats. I worked there from 3 a.m. to 7 a.m.

It was hard work but I managed it OK, and I didn't have any trouble until the end of the week when I got my pay. I was just about to put my $120 in my pocket when a big black guy came to me and said, 'You got to pay $20 protection money.'

'I beg your pardon?' I said.

'Twenty bucks. That's what you owe for protection.'

There was no way I was going to pay anyone $20 of my salary. The guy was standing there, waiting for me to hand over a bill; but instead I took one of the metal hooks used to carry the fish-baskets and I swung this thing at him, smacking it into his face. He fell on the floor yelling in agony, and so I kicked him, and then I ran. That was the end of my career as a dock worker.

After this incident I hurried back to the shop. I needed to get out of town before I got into real trouble, so I grabbed a bag and headed out to the turnpike. I left most of my luggage in storage at the shop.

I decided to reinvent myself as a hippy. I was wearing an overcoat from Saville Row in London; I had Cecil Gee suits and gold bracelets. It was all excellent gear, but I had to admit that I didn't look much like a hippy at this point.

I was also determined to hitch-hike across America. The first leg of my journey took me from New York to Pennsylvania. I passed through Pittsburgh and Harrisburg, and I connected with the hippies wherever I went and wherever I could find them. I think it was a bit of a novelty for them, having a Chinese guy in an English suit hanging around with them. There was a lot of drug-taking and sex – 'free love', as it was known –

but I was used to drugs and sex. After all, we had *ganja* in Singapore, and I had been familiar with some of the hostesses. So I moved into a world of lust and dope, and I found that it suited me very well. The guys I mixed with would listen to music by Emerson, Lake and Palmer, Genesis, and Alice Cooper. If I could find a place to stay, I would make that my base for a couple of weeks before I moved on again.

I'd got as far as Brunswick, Ohio when I met up with Billy and Bugsy. I was just strolling along the road, thumbing for a lift, when a brightly coloured van pulled up beside me. The window wound down and a guy with long hair and a beard shouted out to me, 'Hey, man, where are you heading?'

'Nowhere, dude!' I said.

'Come and stay with us at the commune! We live just near here in Brunswick.'

The driver introduced himself as Roger. He had a passenger with him, a quiet, skinny guy whose name was Roman. Roger was married to a girl called Cathy; they were very young, just 18 or 19. They lived with Roman and Roger's brother-in-law Billy. I accepted their kind invitation and ended up at Roger and Cathy's house. Roger's father had bought him the house and visited every Saturday night with groceries for everyone. He would stay over to see how things were and would then leave on the Sunday morning.

That evening they had a big party to celebrate foreigners in general and me in particular. I told them I was on the run, and that seemed to make them like me even more.

I remember the way these guys used to organize drinks at their parties. They would get a really big pot and then whoever came to the party just poured whatever drink they had into the pot. Some people brought

LSD along and they put that in the pot as well. By the time a party was in full swing they had quite a wicked mixture in that bowl! I didn't know this at the time; I thought they were just making some kind of punch.

I had a cup of this stuff, thinking it was a fairly mild alcoholic drink. I was sitting next to Billy and Bugsy and they were playing some acid rock music; someone had strung some purple lights across the room and everyone was just chilled. Then after about twenty minutes I noticed that the room was moving! The whole place was spinning around. I looked at my hands; it seemed like my palms were coming up at me even though they weren't moving. I knew what alcohol could do to someone, and this did not feel like alcohol.

'What's happening to me, man?' I said to Bugs.

'Man, you're on acid!' he said and laughed.

I thought he meant real acid – sulphuric or hydrochloric!

'What? Acid?' I said, panicking.

'Yeah, man,' said Bugsy, laughing at me again.

I ran into the bathroom and made myself sick, and then some drank water. Then I went to the kitchen and drank some milk.

After about fifteen minutes I went back to Bugsy.

'Hey, man, is this stuff going to burn a hole through me?' I asked him nervously.

'No – it's not that kind of acid,' he said. 'It's LSD. You're just tripping.'

'Oh, OK,' I said. 'That's fine.'

But it wasn't fine. I didn't like the experience. I felt nervous and out of control. I also noticed that this 'trip' was making me hungry. I decided that I really wanted to get something to eat, so I called to Garry, one of the other guys at the party. I knew he had some transport.

'Tell you what,' I said, 'give me a lift to Cleveland and we'll get some Chinese.'

'Sure,' he said.

So we drove out to Cleveland. We were both tripping and it was a crazy journey. The road swayed around, and the other vehicles seemed to glide into each other. I'm amazed we didn't have an accident.

Garry pulled up outside the restaurant and I went in and ordered the food. I forgot that I was supposed to be getting takeaway and so I sat down and got ready to eat whatever they put in front of me. The waiter brought some roast duck and put it on the table; but when I looked at the plate, the duck started running across the table!

'Waiter!' I waved frantically.

'Yes, sir?' said the waiter, looking bemused.

'How much is it? I must pay you!' I said, digging into my pocket.

I dumped some notes on the table and dashed back out to the car.

'You all right, buddy?' said Garry. He was so stoned on LSD that he had forgotten why we had come out.

'Sure. Come on, let's go back,' I said, and we just drove back to the party.

We got back to discover that the other guys had run out of booze, so we walked down to the corner store to buy more. A couple from Korea, Mr and Mrs Yi, ran the store, keeping it open pretty much all the time. Mrs Yi (or 'May', as she was called) usually worked in the shop.

On this occasion we were disappointed. The shop was shut and would not be opening again until the next day. Roger wanted to get some more drink, so in the end we got on the freeway and headed towards Dallas to get some beer. We went about twenty miles, decided that the whole thing was a crazy idea, turned round and then came back.

I was still feeling the effects of the LSD, and I didn't stop tripping for about sixteen hours. I was exhausted when I came down and I slept for ages afterwards. It was a bizarre and horrible experience, but I still came back and did it again and again. Neither did we confine ourselves to LSD. One day Roger came home with some aeroplane glue. We knew that glue could have a hallucinogenic effect, so we decided to try it out. We sniffed this stuff and I ended up getting so high that for some reason I took off my spectacles and broke them into pieces. I didn't really know what was going on.

When I came down I thought, *What the hell happened to me? What was I doing?*

In the midst of all this hippy hedonism, Roger and Cathy had a little baby and they called her Kelly. They went to the local church to get her baptized, and they asked me to be her godfather; I was happy to oblige. As I write this, I am thinking about the fact that Kelly must now be 36 years old!

Roger and I were always experimenting. We once tried to do some home-made tattoos. My star sign is Aries, and so I tried to create an Aries tattoo on my arm.

Roger's dad gave him some financial support, but I think even he got fed up with the situation in the end. He came round one day and said he wasn't going to do this any more; Roger would have to find a job.

I left Roger and Cathy's house and ended up living with Billy and Bugsy, where I continued to be something of a novelty for their friends – a Chinaman from Singapore living in Brunswick, Ohio! Bugsy's mother even took me to the school where she taught, to talk to the children about Singapore.

One of the kids said to me, 'My mummy is on her own; you could come and be my daddy. My mummy would love you.'

It was a tempting offer, but I stayed with Bugsy and Billy. Life was quite simple for me at this time; I had no involvement with the gangs, and I lived on some money that I had brought with me from New York. I still didn't have a job, but sometimes Billy would give me some money. These guys respected me and treated me like an honoured guest.

Sometimes my background and experience came in handy. There was one occasion when we were having a Chinese meal in a restaurant. We were minding our own business, and across the way from us was a group of American kids. With them was a young Chinese guy from the local karate club, and they described him as their 'master'. The group of kids taunted my friends, winding them up and getting them agitated. They were calling out to our group, 'Our master is better than your master!' – by which, of course, they meant me!

It looked like things were going to get out of hand, so I went over to their 'master' and spoke to him in Mandarin Chinese:

'Look,' I said, 'let's have peace; there's no point in having a fight. You don't want to have a fight with me and I don't want to have a fight with you.'

'I agree,' he said. 'I'm just here to have a meal, but these guys have got themselves a bit over-excited.'

'We'd better make up some story to convince them that it's not worth fighting about,' I said.

After some more discussion we told all of the kids that we had actually learned from the same master, and that this made us like brothers, and so we would not fight. It was complete nonsense, of course, but they were impressed.

I continued to enjoy my popularity with my hippy friends. I was just so different, and they loved it! I was a Chinese guy travelling the world, dressed in a suit like some kind of mafioso.

While I was staying with Billy and Bugsy I discovered that not everyone liked me. The only person I really had any trouble with was Ronnie, and it was at about this time that I had my various encounters with him. After we had had our little game of Russian roulette, I knew that he would not bother me again, but that experience unsettled me and I decided that it was time to move on. I had enjoyed staying with Billy and Bugsy, but my aim had always been to keep travelling, all the way to California. So I continued to work my way westwards across the continent.

At Salt Lake City a military guy picked me up. He said he was going to Vietnam and he drove me as far as Dallas. When he dropped me off he gave me $275 – a massive sum in those days. He was going back to Vietnam after a period of rest and recreation, and he said he didn't need the money. There was an air of resignation about him, like he wasn't expecting to come back to his country again. I have no idea whether he came back, and at the time I was unnerved by his fatalistic approach. It reminded me of the unease that I felt about my own life and my purpose on earth.

Somewhere between Chicago and Salt Lake City I walked into a truck stop. It was quite late, about 10.30 p.m., I was tired, and I had nowhere to stay. I sat in the corner drinking coffee and looking miserable. The lady who ran the truck stop took pity on me; she cooked herself a meal and she gave me half of it. Then she said that I could sleep in the corner and she would wake me up when she finished her shift in the morning. I made my bed in the corner of the truck stop and settled down to sleep.

A few hours later, with the sun rising outside, she woke me and cooked me breakfast. Then she made me steak sandwiches and a drink for the journey, gave me a lift down to the freeway and then, when I got out of the car, she gave me $20. I will never forget her kindness. It made such an impression on me that when I got to California I sent her some flowers to say thank you – a very uncommon gesture of gratitude for me at that time.

6

The Golden State, and Back Again

A journey of a thousand miles begins with a single step.

Confucius

I reached California in the New Year of 1972. I'd made it from one side of the continent to the other, and I felt a great sense of achievement as I crossed the state line. I had not lost the knack of making new contacts; I'd made friends with a Chinese student when I was in Chicago and he had given me the contact details of some of his friends in California. They were the people I got in touch with first.

I ended up meeting a young student called Vincent Heep who was living in Los Angeles. Vincent was a very clever guy; he was working on a doctorate in astrophysics when I met him. I stayed at his place while I went out to look for work, and I quickly managed to get an interview for a job at an air-crew training company in Los Angeles. I went to the office to fill out forms and joined a group of other interviewees.

I quickly realized that I had a problem. The other candidates were smartly dressed and had attaché cases with them. I was still in the clothes I had worn as I crossed America: my suit was scruffy, I had a stubbly beard and

I had not had a haircut in months. Even the office secretary looked at me with contempt.

The boss came out of his office and looked at the array of candidates, finishing with me. 'Would you mind waiting to be the last one to be interviewed?' he asked.

'No, that's fine,' I said. What else could I say? I wanted the job.

I was supposed to have an interview at 2.30 p.m. but it was 6.30 before it was my turn. The receptionist had gone; the other candidates had gone; everybody had gone! The boss came out, apologized for keeping me waiting, and invited me into his office. As I walked in I noticed that there was a piece of screwed-up paper on the floor. It was placed in quite a prominent position so that anyone who walked in would have noticed it. As I followed him in, he walked by this piece of paper and completely ignored it. I reached down and picked it up.

'Excuse me,' I said. 'Do you have a wastepaper basket here?'

'Why do you want that?' he asked.

'There is a piece of litter here on the floor, and I wanted to throw it away,' I replied.

He smiled and took the screwed-up piece of paper from me and invited me to sit down.

'Now then,' he said, sitting back and staring at me, 'why should I give you this job? I'm sure you saw all those immaculately dressed guys out there earlier that I interviewed, and I'm sure you know you need a shave and a haircut. So what can you offer?'

'You should employ me,' I said, 'because I'm positive and diligent, and I will produce results. I can sell!'

Then before he could reply, I continued with my sales pitch:

'I tell you what – I won't want a penny off you,' I said. 'Try me out for two weeks and we'll see if things work out. You'll see my results and then you can tell me how much you are going to pay me after that. Otherwise we don't owe each other anything. Is that a deal?'

He looked at me and smiled again. 'I will give you a call. Thank you for coming in,' he said.

I left thinking that this had been a short but successful interview. The next day he did indeed call me. 'You were very good, Mr Goh. You've got the job,' he said. 'Do you want to know why?'

'Because I was able to sell myself to you effectively,' I replied.

'Well, that was part of it,' he said, 'but it was also because when you walked in, you picked up a piece of paper on the floor. You were only the second person to do that. The other person who did it was a Chicano, an elderly Mexican-American guy. The others thought they were too good for that – it wasn't their job. I purposely put it there to see how many people would pick it up. Now, when can you come back to the office?'

'Anytime,' I replied.

'Come tomorrow,' he said. 'See the receptionist and take the key for Room Number 4, then come and see me.'

The next day I turned up at the office, still with long hair, still in scruffy clothes, and the same receptionist who had stared at me just two days before was sitting at her desk.

'What do you want?' she said, rather abruptly. Clearly, she didn't know that I'd been given the position.

'I want the key to Room Number 4,' I said. 'And it's "Mr Goh" to you – I got the job!'

I went into my office and then I went to see my new boss, whose name was Tom. He looked me up and down for a moment, and was clearly not impressed with what he saw.

'We need to smarten you up,' he said. Then he gave me an authorization to withdraw $200 and sent me to the company cashier.

'Go out and get a haircut and a new change of clothes and then come back to me,' he said. So that's what I did. I returned a couple of hours later in a new suit and a smart haircut – and then I got on with the business of selling air-crew training.

Although I was new to the business, I was very successful. After about three weeks the boss came by my office and told me to come and see him. I went up to his room and found that one of my colleagues, a Mexican guy, had been called in too.

'I've just fired two of my staff,' said Tom. 'One of them was based in Hawaii and the other one in San Diego. I am promoting you both to their positions, but you need to decide which place each of you wants to go to.'

My colleague, Daniel, didn't want to be too far from his family, so he chose San Diego. That suited me just fine; the idea of spending some time working in Hawaii sounded good to me. I packed my things and got on the plane and started my new job there in the spring of 1972.

I did a good job and we had a steady trade selling training for flight crews to the airlines who worked the routes in and out of Hawaii. During this time I visited lots of bars, slept with lots of women, and tried to convince myself that I really was having a good time. I tried to ignore the nagging feeling somewhere inside me that this was not the best way to live life; the feeling that, despite all the fun I was having, somehow something was missing.

I was in a bar one day and I met a short, fat guy in his late forties who introduced himself as Mr Pan. He started to talk to me about properties in Florida. Apparently there was a building boom there at this time and a lot of people were trying to make money out of the situation. He sounded very knowledgeable on the subject, but because I was pretty experienced as a con man I sensed that he might be trying to con me; there was something about the way he described the deal that made me real-ize what he was really all about. I suspected that it was a sting to make money out of people, but I decided to play along.

I told him that I was from a big organization in Singapore and that my family was involved in banking; so naturally he got quite excited about the prospect of doing business with me. He was very keen for me to get my family in Singapore to invest in these properties. Our relationship developed and I started to change cheques with him; I would write a cheque to him for cash and he would do the same for me. We kept changing cheques for different amounts; and I always made sure that my cheques were honoured at the bank. Quite often I would go over to his house and we would get drunk together; and all this time he was hoping that the incredibly rich banking family I had invented for myself would put a lot of money into his 'investment properties' in Florida.

This carried on for a few months, and I spent more and more time with this guy. He thought I was working up to a big investment, but the main thing on my mind was learning his signature. I stayed at his place quite a few times, even sleeping in his office where he kept his financial papers – and his chequebook. He thought he was going to con me, but I was the one who was going to sting him, and I knew that when I did, I would have to leave Hawaii and my job.

When the time was right, I arranged one last visit to his house. It was a Sunday night, and as usual I slept in his office. In the morning I took his chequebook and tore out just one blank cheque. I took it from somewhere near the bottom of the chequebook. I said goodbye to him that morning and headed off to the bank. I'd already made arrangements to leave Hawaii. I went to the bank, forged Mr Pan's signature, and wrote out a cheque for $50,000 – that's about a quarter of a million dollars in today's money. I told the cashier that I'd take $40,000 in cash and then put $10,000 into my bank account. The cashier conferred with the supervisor, and I tried to look calm as I waited for them to finish talking. Eventually the cashier returned and cashed the cheque. When I left the bank I went straight to the travel agent and bought a flight to Portugal, paying for the ticket with cash. I did not mind leaving Hawaii; I was getting bored anyway by that stage. Girls and drink were all very well, but I felt that it was time for me to move on.

The flight had a one-night stop-over in LA. When we touched down at the airport I phoned my boss and we went out for dinner. I told him I was leaving and he said that he was sad to see me go, but actually he was having some problems himself and was also planning to leave the company. We had a good dinner and parted as friends.

I stayed one night in Los Angeles and then I got on the plane to fly to New York. I bought a separate ticket so that it would be more difficult for Mr Pan, or any of his associates, to find me. I didn't know how he would react to the loss of $50,000 but I could imagine what might happen if he managed to track me down.

I took a Jumbo to New York – an old-style 747 with a bar in the upstairs deck. Once we were in the air I went up to get a drink, and as usual I started to work my charm. I got chatting to a Jewish guy who looked like he was intending to spend the whole of the flight at the bar. He was very well dressed and so I started to talk to him. He bought me a drink and we talked and drank our way to New York. By the time we got there we were good friends. He told me his name was Harvey Samuels, and he was a clothing manufacturer; that explained the expertly tailored suit he was wearing. We swapped stories and opinions as the plane made its way eastwards across the continent; and when we landed in New York he asked me if I would like to go to his private club for a massage to unwind after the long trip.

'That would be great,' I said. 'I just need to check into a hotel somewhere.'

'No problem,' said Harvey. 'I'll get my secretary to book you into the Park Sheraton and arrange for your luggage to be delivered there.'

This is great! I thought. *I've only just touched down in New York, and already someone is looking after me.*

We went out to his club and I had a sauna and massage. I'd never felt so good after a flight. I was relaxed, I felt clean, and I was looking forward to taking up Harvey's invitation to visit his office. When we arrived he showed me into a room full of clothes.

'Here's my company's range,' he said. 'Why don't you take anything you want, so you've got some decent outfits?'

'Thank you very much!' I said, and proceeded to pick out a safari suit, an ordinary suit, a few new shirts, and some trousers. When I left him I had to go and buy a new case to carry it all.

I had dinner with someone else that evening – a vice chairman of ITT whose son I had met in Hawaii. The son had asked me to take something back to his dad in New York. We went to the Empire State Building and he bought me dinner in the restaurant at the top. Then, because ITT owned the Park Sheraton, he arranged for me to have a free stay there.

I returned to my free accommodation that first evening feeling very pleased with myself. I'd got across

America the hard way – hitch-hiking along the high-ways and sleeping rough – but I'd come back in style, drinking my way back to the Big Apple on the top deck of a 747, and talking myself into some new sets of clothes and a luxury stay at one of the city's finest hotels. And I still had $40,000 in cash in my pocket.

7

A Night on the Town

Money made through dishonest practices will not last long.

Chinese proverb

Stealing that kind of money can make your life danger-
ous. I didn't really know how much Mr Pan would be
prepared to do to get back the money; or even what he
would do simply to exact his revenge on me. I'd bought
separate tickets from Hawaii to LA, LA to New York,
and New York to Portugal, paying cash to help cover my
tracks; but I couldn't allow my luxurious surroundings
in the Big Apple to lull me into a false sense of security.
Mr Pan was not the only person I would want to avoid;
after all, the reason I left New York the last time was
because I had just smacked one of the dock gang members with a fish-hook.

Sitting in my hotel room at the Park Sheraton, I
accepted the fact that I could not stay long. With some
reluctance I checked out of the hotel and headed, again,
for the airport.

The flight was uneventful. No upstairs bar and no
interesting characters to talk to. Things got a little more
interesting once the plane had landed, though. I was at
the taxi rank, waiting to get a ride into the centre of

Lisbon, and I noticed that there was also a young lady there trying to get a taxi. I'd managed to secure one, but she was still waiting, and so I invited her to share a taxi with me into town. She was very grateful and proceeded to tell me all about herself.

The accent told me immediately that she was American; her name was Mandy and she was an air hostess with TWA. She was currently on holiday and planning to meet her boyfriend here in Lisbon. I wasn't too happy to hear about the boyfriend, but she was very nice company for the drive into the centre of the city.

I took her to a hotel and dropped her off and went to my hotel, having arranged to pick her up later and take her out for dinner. Fortunately for me, her boyfriend did not turn up and she was very upset. She had had a telex from him saying he was not able to meet her because of unfinished business but he would see her in Casablanca. They had been planning to travel on to Casablanca together from Portugal.

I took her out and wined and dined her, and we became good friends as the evening progressed. After the meal we jumped into a taxi and headed back to her hotel, necking in the car all the way there. We walked into the hotel reception and I was certain that my luck was in.

I was just about to head up the stairs when the guy on reception stepped out in front of me: 'I'm sorry, sir. You cannot go up there as well.'

I looked at him in amazement, and then said, 'OK, here's $50. I'd like a room, please.'

'I'm sorry, sir,' he said. 'I cannot sell you a room.'

So I put $100 down and said, 'Now I want the best room in the hotel, please!'

Still he refused. I was amazed. I concluded that this was something to do with his Roman Catholic principles.

'I am sorry, sir,' he said, 'you will have to come back tomorrow.' He looked me in the eye and I decided not to make an issue of it. I gave her a goodnight kiss and arranged to see her in the morning.

When I got back to my own hotel I was really upset and told the porter there all about it.

'You should have brought her back here,' he said, laughing. 'I would have let her stay here!'

'Thanks,' I said ruefully. I don't know why I hadn't thought of that at the time; maybe I was just a little too drunk to work it out.

The following morning I met her and we went on a tour around Lisbon. All the time I was aware of the fact that she would be leaving for Casablanca that evening, and so I would not get a chance to spend the night with her. We had a wonderful day together and I met her later at the ferry to say goodbye. She told me that she thought her boyfriend still might not turn up.

'Here,' I said, passing over a piece of paper, 'telex me at this number in Madrid in a couple of days' time, OK?'

I knew then that if she did send me a message, and the boyfriend didn't materialize, I'd be heading for Casablanca immediately.

I went back to the hotel and sat in the bar, drowning my sorrows. While I was there, a French guy by the name of Pierre Marceau came in and we started talking. He was an auditor by trade, and he spoke good English. We had some dinner and then went out to a local bar to carry on drinking. I was happy to drink the night away; I needed a distraction after the disappointment with Mandy.

The evening wore on and the bars in Lisbon started to close down for the night, but both of us wanted some more action.

'I've got my car,' he said. 'Why don't we drive out to the casino at Estoril?'

'Sure,' I said. It sounded like a great idea to me.

We drove the twenty kilometres or so out to the casino and found that, like the rest of Portugal by this time of night, the place was shut. We finally admitted defeat and headed back to the hotel, passing a number of firmly closed bars on the way.

'I tell you what,' I said to Pierre. 'Let's meet tomorrow evening and drink the nightcap that we were not able to drink this evening.'

'That sounds good to me,' he said.

So I met up with Pierre the next evening and we decided to give the casino another try. We jumped in his Renault and made our way out of Lisbon again towards Estoril. This time the casino was open and we ordered a large cognac each. We weren't planning on going to the tables to gamble, and as we looked around the bar we both noticed a stunningly beautiful girl sitting nearby. She had blonde hair and blue eyes, and as I stared at her Pierre leaned over to me and said, 'I bet you can't pull her, Bobby.'

I smiled and put down my drink. 'You shouldn't bet with me, my friend,' I said. 'I like a challenge, and when it involves a pretty girl, I can't resist!'

There was a guy already sitting with her, chatting her up, but that didn't put me off. They certainly didn't look like they were together. I took my drink and my packet of cigarettes and I just plonked myself down opposite her. I could see she had a lighter, so I asked her if I could borrow it.

The guy sitting with her turned out to be an American, and she was from South Africa. She told me her name was Giselle. He was telling her stories from the USA, but I was able to trump anything he said because of my experiences there as well as in other parts of the world. Pretty soon after that he made his excuses and left. As he departed, my friend Pierre arrived.

'So what brings you here?' I asked her.

'I'm waiting for my mother,' replied Giselle. 'She's in there gambling at the moment.' She nodded towards the main area of the casino.

'Have you had dinner yet?' Pierre asked her.

'No,' she replied, 'but if you can find my mother and bring her out of there, I'll come with you for dinner.'

I left Giselle in the care of Pierre and went into the casino to find the mother. With hindsight, I realize that I should have sent him in to find her mother, but I decided to play the hero.

The first thing I had to do was buy some chips for the casino, because no one was allowed into the gambling hall unless they had first bought a few chips.

So I bought $50 worth and went in to find the mother. It was very crowded and I couldn't see anyone who fitted her description. I wandered around, trying to ignore the lure of the games going on all around me. The mother was nowhere to be seen, and I eventually succumbed to a dice game. Just as the dice were being thrown, the guy who was sitting in front of me stood up and walked away, so as an automatic reaction I went and sat down! I was just going to blow this $50 and then find the mother and get out, that was all.

* * * *

Three hours later I lost $20,000, and I only stopped because I had practically run out of money. I looked up at the clock, and I remembered why I had gone in there in the first place. I would not have been surprised to find that both Giselle and Pierre had left me behind.

But when I got back to the bar I found them still waiting, with Giselle's mother, whom I had failed to locate. They'd bought some sandwiches while they were waiting for me to come back. I can't remember what I said to them then, but I know that I walked into the casino with $20,000 and I walked out with 500 escudos – that's about $450. If I'd had the other $20,000 with me, I would have blown the whole lot. I didn't even get a chance to take the South African girl back to my hotel. It was another miserable end to an evening in Lisbon.

The following day I said goodbye to Pierre and headed to the airport for my flight to Madrid. I had made an appointment to see someone there, a Norwegian guy called Uli Ondall whom I had met at the hotel in New York. He was trying to get some money together to buy out his father-in-law's business, and I figured that, one way or another, I was going to profit from the deal.

While I was in Madrid I received a telex from Mandy to say that her boyfriend had arrived – but if I wanted to join them I could. I had no intention of doing that, of course, and now I focused on some business arrangements with my Norwegian acquaintance.

I retreated to the hotel bar – a favourite haunt of mine – and began to think about what I was going to do next. I was deep in thought when I heard someone call my name:

'Hey, Bobby, how are ya?' I heard the familiar, broad, American-Italian accent and I thought, *That's my old friend Mario from New York!*

'Hey, Mario!' I turned and smiled, genuinely pleased to meet him again. 'Good to see you! How's business?'

'Well, you know what,' he said, 'I figure it's nearly time for me to retire – put my feet up and enjoy life a little – you know?'

'Sure,' I said. I didn't know how old Mario was, but I guessed he had been involved in business with the Families for many years.

'I'm looking forward to a few quiet years back in Sicily. I'm on my way there now to have a look at some of the old family properties.'

I nodded as he ordered a drink from the bar.

'You know what, Bobby,' he continued. 'If you ever find yourself in Sicily you should drop by and visit me, yes?' He passed me a card with a phone number on it.

'I'd like that, Mario – thanks,' I said, making a point to remember his offer. It was always good to have an invitation to stay in different parts of the world.

Over the next couple of weeks I met with Uli frequently, talking business and spinning stories for him. We had a good time, but I knew that I had to move on. I told him that I was going to Switzerland to sort out some business for him. I didn't really con the guy; he just gave me some hospitality. I don't know what happened to him after that.

So from Madrid I travelled on to Paris. I was still nervous about the possibility of Mr Pan tracking me down, so again I paid cash for a rail ticket. From Paris I travelled straight on down to the south of France and ended up at the Grand Hotel in Marseilles. I struck up a friendship with the proprietor straight away. He took me out for dinner with his family, and with them I learnt how to drink crème de menthe, a sweet, mint-flavoured liqueur.

From there I travelled on to Italy, again by train, and finished up in Milan, and as usual I stayed in an expensive hotel. Once I'd checked in I went for a walk and immediately noticed some auction rooms, quite near to the hotel. I decided that it was time for me to get into the art business.

I went to one of the auctions and walked confidently in, trying to radiate as much bravado as I could. I still had some cheques from my Hawaiian bank account and I used these to 'buy' some of the paintings at the auction. I gave instructions for the pieces to be parcelled up and sent to my old address in Hawaii. I thoroughly enjoyed spending a non-existent fortune during a busy morning of trading at the auction house.

At lunchtime the manager approached me and offered to buy me lunch. How could I refuse? My cheques were not going to bounce for a few days, and until then I was a respectable art dealer and I enjoyed being treated as such. The lunch was very good and the champagne proved to be an excellent vintage. We talked art and I tried to act as if I knew what I was talking about.

After a couple of days I moved on to Genoa and found the best hotel I could. I ate there that evening and the head waiter started chatting with me.

'You come out with me tomorrow night, yes?' he said to me with a big smile.

'Sure!' I said. It sounded like fun to me.

The next evening we headed out to a bar owned by one of his friends, tucked away down one of the little side streets. We had a good evening and we chatted and I bought some drinks, but when the bill came I discovered that I was being charged $500. It was an exorbitant amount! I knew that there was no way I had ordered that much drink, and I realized that I had been conned.

When this sort of thing happened, not only would I get annoyed about having to pay out a lot of money, but my professional pride was also hurt. I was the con man! I was the one who swindled others out of their money, not the other way round. When other people tried to do it to me I just felt indignant.

I told the bar owner that I would not be able to get that kind of money until Monday, when the local American Express office opened.

'I tell you what,' I said, 'here is a cheque for $500. You can hold onto that, and on Monday we will go to the Amex office and we can cash it then, and you will have your money.'

I was careful to hide my indignation, promising to return the following evening for another session at the bar.

The next night, Saturday night, I came back again with the waiter and we had a ball. I bought cigars and drinks; I even hired a couple of local prostitutes and had sex with these girls before I came back to the bar again. I paid for all of this through the bar and when the bill came, this time it was $2,300.

'Hey,' I said, 'I feel great; this has been a wonderful party. I will give you another cheque, and let's make it $3,000, and you can give me the rest in liras.'

The bar manager accepted my cheque and gave me the equivalent of $700 in liras. Just to prove how generous I was, I gave $100 worth of liras to the head waiter and $50 worth of liras each to the prostitutes. Then, happy and drunk, I headed back to the hotel.

I knew that the waiter did not work on Sunday morning, and so quite early the next day I packed my bags, slipped out of the hotel and went to the train station, leaving behind a couple of guys who thought they had conned me. They would soon realize who had been conned when they discovered that the cheques were not worth the paper they were written on.

8

The Diplomatic Service

If you have money, you can make the ghosts and devils turn your grindstone.

Chinese proverb

It was another quiet exit from yet another country. This time I decided to take the train to Zurich in Switzerland. I hoped that this civilized and affluent town, set beside a beautiful lake, would offer me some opportunities for employment, or a con – or both.

In the end, another opportunity came to me even before I had arrived. As we crossed over the border I went to the buffet carriage to get some food, and I also purchased a copy of the *Herald Tribune*. As I leafed through the job pages, one particular ad caught my eye:

REQUIRED: housekeeper and domestic help for the residence of the First Secretary of the Australian Consulate in Cologne.

That was going to be my next job.

When the train pulled into the station at Zurich I went straight to a phone-booth and called the number in the ad. Eventually I was put through to the First Secretary, who introduced himself as Mr Brogan.

'I am phoning about the job in the *Herald Tribune*,' I said. 'You need a housekeeper and domestic help.'

There was a pause at the other end of the line.

'I was looking for a woman,' said the voice.

I was ready for this objection; I had already thought about what I would say to counter it.

'Why do you need a woman?' I asked. 'I can cook, I can clean, I can sew. Why don't you give me a chance?'

Mr Brogan did not sound convinced but he agreed to see me.

'Where are you?' he asked.

'In Switzerland,' I replied. 'I can come to you now; I'll get on the train and come straight away.'

He agreed to see me, and so I bought a single ticket for Cologne. When I arrived I went straight from the station to the Consulate for my interview. After my experience with the air-crew training company in Los Angeles, I was confident that I would get the job.

The interview went well. I was able to persuade him that I could do anything a woman could do, and so he hired me.

It transpired that Mr Brogan was a bachelor but he did have a fiancée. His family had moved to Australia from Cork many years ago, and he still retained a trace of Irish accent. He showed me a map of Ireland with all the different family names and we chatted about his ancestry. On my first day in his employment he called me up to his room.

'Can you shoot?' he asked.

'Yes, I can,' I said, truthfully. He opened a door in his bedside cabinet and took out a revolver. He passed the weapon to me.

'If anyone forces their way into the house, just shoot them, OK?'

'Sure,' I said. From that moment I knew that I would enjoy working for Mr Brogan – he was my kind of guy. Fortunately none of the local crooks ever broke into the place; I would have had no hesitation in using the gun.

Mr Brogan did not smoke but he did drink. He had a big bottle of Courvoisier in the shape of a cannon, and pretty soon we got into the routine of having a drink in the evening when he was home from the Consulate.

'If there's anything you want, tell my secretary,' he said.

I was smoking every day and eventually he started too. He and I sat in his house in the evening smoking and drinking cognac, and he told me his life story and some of his current responsibilities.

He was involved in the drafting of the Geneva Convention and his work would take him to Geneva for weeks at a time. I thought I would have to do a lot of cooking for him, but in the end I only needed to do it once, when he had the Canadian First Secretary and his wife over for dinner. Other than that I just looked after his house, did some washing and kept him company.

One evening Mr Brogan came home and opened his post as usual. One envelope contained a short, hand-written letter and a press cutting. He read the letter. I could see that he was shocked by its contents, so I just sat and waited for him to tell me what had happened. He passed me the press cutting. It was a wedding photo, but I did not recognize either half of the happy couple.

'See that girl,' he said.

'Yes.'

'That's my fiancée. She's gone and married another man.'

I looked at him and he went on, 'The letter is from my family, telling me about it. I had no idea,' he said, sitting down, 'no idea.'

I reached for the bottle of Courvoisier – we were in for a long night.

* * * *

On those occasions when Mr Brogan had to travel to Switzerland, he arranged to retain me on half salary, and then he would buy me a ticket and tell me I could go anywhere I liked in Europe. I was very happy with this arrangement; I got a small income and I could do what I liked, wherever I liked.

An additional perk of the job was the fact that I had a diplomatic pass. This proved to be very useful when I was on my extended holidays.

One time, while Mr Brogan was away mediating in a Middle East peace conference, I visited the town of Mainz. I was looking for a good night out, and during the course of the evening I got drunk as usual. Sat in a crowded bar, I began to feel the heat, and because I was sitting near the entrance, I opened the door to let in a breeze. The problem was, after I had opened the door, one of the German guys at another table got up and shut it. This happened twice.

In the end I confronted the guy: 'Look,' I said, 'you come outside with me and we will settle this.'

He was as drunk as I was, and followed me out of the bar. We had a fight there on the pavement, causing a lot of noise and chaos in the process. The bar owner was pretty unhappy with our antics and called the police. I ended up in a cell at the local police station, where I told the coppers that I was a diplomat. They thought I was just saying that because I was drunk or high on something, so they put me in a cell with another drunk. This was the middle of summer and the heat was oppressive, so I decided to splash my face with some water from a bowl in the cell.

Some of the water fell on this other guy and he started screaming his head off and making all kinds of noise. I told him to be quiet but he would not stop, so I beat him up a bit. He started making even more noise and eventually the coppers came in and took him to another cell.

Early the next morning they hauled me out and asked to see my diplomatic pass. I showed them my papers and the next thing I knew, I was out on the street again looking for a café where I could get some breakfast.

Mr Brogan's absence was a chance for me to relax a bit. On one occasion I found out about a party going on in another town. The travel didn't bother me and I made the journey to the party venue, where I had a great time drinking and charming people, as usual. I got chatting to some US servicemen at the party, and one of them told me that they were flying up to Frankfurt by helicopter the next day.

When the party was over I needed to get back home but I was wrecked, as usual. I wandered out of the party venue and made my way down the street, heading out of town. Pretty soon I found myself at the perimeter of a US Air Force base. I followed the fence around the base until I found a loose section and I was able to wander in undetected. I hadn't been in there long before tiredness overcame me and I fell asleep.

I woke up a few hours later, feeling pretty rough; and I knew that I needed to find a way to get home. I wandered further onto the base and found an office. There was a guy in a tee-shirt sitting at the desk, so I went in.

'Excuse me,' I said, 'I know there's a helicopter flying out to Frankfurt this morning, and I wondered if I could hitch a ride.'

The guy looked at me like he had seen a ghost. 'What?' he shouted. 'Who the heck are you?'

Before I could answer, he pointed to his shoulder. I hadn't seen any indication of his rank but now I could see that he bore the insignia of a US Air Force colonel.

'I'll ask again!' he said. 'Who are you, soldier? What is your rank, and who is your commanding officer?'

I lied and told him that my platoon was out on a field operation and that I had only just arrived from the States, so I was not on official duty yet. I had gained all the necessary information from one of my new American friends. I gave him my friend's name and rank and he then got one of his staff to call the Military Police. A couple of very hard-looking MP guys came over and escorted me to their station. These guys believed my story, and they were intent on reporting me to my 'commanding officer'.

I waited in a military cell for an hour, wondering what would happen to me, and then an MP sergeant came into my cell.

'There's been an accident,' he said. 'You won't be able to get back to Frankfurt till late this evening. What are you in for, solider?'

'I just need to join my platoon,' I said.

The sergeant looked at me like he had better things to do than worry about some grunt solider who just needed to get to the right place.

'Best thing you can do,' he said, 'is to get out of this base and hitch a ride up the autobahn to Frankfurt, otherwise you're gonna spend all day cluttering up the place.'

That was all the encouragement I needed.

'Thank you, sergeant,' I said. 'I'll get out of here right now,' and I made my way out to the gate and then off the base, and eventually back home.

During my time there in Germany it was quite easy to go in and out of a base as long as you spoke with an

American accent and you knew a bit of the lingo. I would walk confidently up to the gate, smiling at everyone. 'Hey, dude, what's happening? Take it easy, man!' These were the phrases that got me onto the site. Once there I'd sleep in the barracks, eat in the canteen, play cards with the guys there, even go to the movies and drink with them. When they went to work in the morning I just used to sleep; and if anyone asked me what I was doing I'd say it was my day off, or I was on shift work.

It was while I was in Germany that I met a Spanish guy called Alberto. He and I just got on well together and we decided to stay in touch. He and his wife liked to go to the flamenco dancing clubs in Cologne. It was through Alberto that I managed to get involved with the German mafia.

During one of Mr Brogan's trips away I decided to visit Zabriggen, near Stuttgart. Alberto had been appointed head chef at a new restaurant in the city, and I tagged along too so that I could give Alberto a hand as his assistant and also supplement my income. I got to know some of the German mafiosi who frequented the place as well as the hostesses who worked there. The local mafia boss owned a bar across the street from the restaurant and we would go drinking there after a shift.

One day I asked one of the mafia guys, 'So where can I go to have a good time in this town?'

'You need to go to the disco,' he said. 'Ralph here will take you.' Ralph was a young lad, about 18 or so; I had met him in the restaurant, where he helped out by collecting plates.

So Ralph took me to the disco, and I took my gun with me. I enjoyed dancing, but I also liked to sit and watch others dance as well. I was sitting in the disco with Ralph, just quietly smoking a pipe of marijuana and minding my own business, when some Middle Eastern or Moroccan guy walked past me on the way to the rest-room, and he accidentally kicked my leg as he did so. He did not apologize.

This was the sort of behaviour that used to irritate me, because it showed a lack of respect. I thought about what I was going to say to this guy, but it was just an accident and so I thought no more about it. A couple of minutes later, when I had calmed down, he came back the other way from the rest-room and as he passed me he kicked my leg again! Now I had to deal with the situation. As he walked away from me I got up with my drink and moved towards him, tapping him hard on the shoulder.

'Why were you kicking me?' I said as he turned.

The guy looked at me and seemed to indicate that he could not understand what I was saying. I guessed he could understand English very well, and I was not impressed by his attempts to put me off. So I pulled out the gun and waved it in front of him. His eyes widened visibly as he saw the barrel pointing at him.

'Now you understand me,' I said. 'Now I will have to treat you like a son who needs to be disciplined. Get down on your knees and say, "Father, I am sorry."'

Still looking at the gun, the Moroccan guy got down on his knees and, while he was down there, I poured my beer over his head. Then I turned him round and kicked his backside; and so honour was restored.

I went back and sat down again with Ralph, who had been watching all this with some amusement. What I didn't realize was that the Moroccan had gone and complained to the management about me. A few minutes later a couple of bouncers came over with the manager and threw us out of the club. In the process Ralph got into a fight with the manager; it was an ugly and embarrassing scene and we were both annoyed about being treated in this way. Full of indignation, we went back to the mafia-owned bar and reported what had happened. Ralph told the whole story in his native German to the guys who were in there, and they decided that something had to be done about the way we had been treated. Again, it was a question of respect.

A few minutes later a team of mafia boys crashed through the entrance of the club, found the manager and beat him up, and then they started shooting the place up. Everyone was back in the bar a short while later, satisfied that the point had been made.

One of the guys phoned the mafia bar owner and told him what had happened. He was furious and put in a call to his brother, who happened to be the Police Commissioner for the area. The Commissioner sent a squad over to the disco to arrest the manager who, I understand, eventually got sacked.

I was a guest at a lot of bars owned by the mafia people, and this was a time of gaining favours and connections. I ended up with a lot of the girls who were hostesses at these bars and I even met some CIA people. I never did any business with any of the CIA, we were just acquaintances. We never discussed business either – I did not want to know about what they were up to.

I stayed in touch with Alberto, and when he moved to Minorca to take up a position as a chef in a hotel there, I decided to say my farewells to Mr Brogan and move there with Alberto. We got on well with the owner of the hotel but not with the General Manager or the Bar Manager. The General Manager didn't like the idea that we were going to run the kitchens the way we wanted to, and no one was going to tell us what to do. I don't know why the Bar Manager didn't like us, but he never gave us any free drinks.

Deprived of any alcohol to help us get through each shift, we decided to raid the spirits store. Our excuse was that we needed a lot of spirits to cook with; and so we ended up with our own bar in the kitchen. We took so much stuff that the General Manager came down to see what was going on.

'Why have you got all this spirit down here in the kitchen?' he asked.

'We need it for the cooking,' I said.

'You're lying!' he shouted. 'You're stealing the hotel's drinks. Both of you!'

'You think so?' I said, angry at his accusations. 'I tell you what, mate. If you come down here and make trouble again, I will come to you with a meat cleaver – got it?'

The General Manager stormed off and had a long discussion with the hotel owner. The owner, who liked us, came and had a chat and we persuaded him that we really did need all of these bottles of alcohol for some of the special sauces that we were making.

After that we never gave the General Manager or the Bar Manager any food from the kitchen. It was not long before he decided that it was best to be nice to us, and normal arrangements were resumed. The General Manager and the Bar Manager got meals from the kitchen, and we got drinks from the bar.

It was a good arrangement from my point of view, but soon Alberto decided to move on, and so I thought that it was time for me to move on as well. I made the short journey from Minorca to Majorca.

I visited a number of different bars once I had arrived, and I soon made friends with a guy called Kurt and his wife. He owned a bar called 'The Rustic Inn'. Kurt and I got on well together and I would drink at the inn from time to time. I found the people there quite easy to get on with, and I made friends with a guy called Gerry who was from the island of Jersey.

On one occasion I was having a party in my flat and Gerry came in looking quite upset.

'Hey, Gerry,' I said, 'what's the problem?'

'Kurt's wife got punched in the face!' he said, clearly shocked by what had happened. 'Some Spanish and Swedish blokes tried to chat her up and then one punched her in the face and broke her glasses!'

Of course, I was outraged. It was bad enough having a friend of mine attacked, but his wife! I grabbed a mate of mine called Marlon and we went down to the bar where the incident was supposed to have happened. Marlon was a captain in the US Air Force and he was a big guy. We could not see anyone who might have done this, and Kurt's wife wasn't there either. Feeling frustrated, we went back to my flat and carried on with the party.

The following night I was at a disco with Gerry and we were dancing around and enjoying ourselves, and then Gerry stopped suddenly and pointed at a group of lads dancing some distance away from us.

'Hey,' he said to me, 'you see those lads over there? They are the people who beat up Kurt's wife.'

I approached these guys and thumped one of them to get their attention.

'You lot beat up the wife of one of my friends last night,' I said. 'We are going to sort this out now. Come on outside.'

So we went outside and I was expecting Gerry to join me, but when I got out there Gerry was beating a quick retreat up the road. All I could see in front of me were about seven or eight Spanish and Swedish guys looking bemused and angry; and then there was me on my own.

I decided to bluff it, and so picked the biggest guy out of all of them, and I said, 'You and me, come on – let's sort this out!' Then I said, 'On second thoughts, I'll take on all of you. Come on, then!' I got into position, ready to take them all on.

But instead of coming at me one of them simply said, 'What's the problem?'

I pointed to Gerry, who was now disappearing into the distance. 'That guy says you beat up my friend's wife,' I said.

'Who?'

'That guy running up the street.' By now Gerry was practically a figure on the horizon.

'We didn't beat up anyone's wife!' said one of them indignantly. 'Who does he think he is, saying this sort of thing!'

And with that they started running after Gerry. He had a good head start on them, but I could see that they were quicker than he was. As they chased after Gerry, I ran back to my flat and got my machetes. When I came back out I couldn't find either these guys or Gerry, and the whole thing seemed to be descending into farce.

The following night I was in this disco again and these guys all turned up, and this time they had brought their three Japanese martial arts teachers with them. They were clearly expecting these teachers to fight with me. I thought I was going to be in for even more trouble, but then I realized that I knew these Japanese guys. I was their friend because I had met them at a restaurant on the island. I started to talk to them, explaining what had happened.

'Look, guys,' I said, 'there's been some misunder-standing. Now, I don't want to fight with you, and I don't suppose you want to fight with me, so let's just make peace, yes?' I mentioned the names of one or two famous Japanese Masters that I said I had trained with, and this seemed to earn me some respect with them. The martial arts teachers nodded and turned to the group who had brought them.

'This man,' they indicated me, 'is our Master's good friend, and so we will not fight with him. You will give respect.'

None of this was quite true, but at least it helped to defuse the situation. The Swedish and Spanish guys looked at me in amazement, but did not argue.

I met an English couple in Kurt's bar; their names were John and Tania Townsend, and they were from Yorkshire. We became friends and I spent a lot of time in the bar drinking with them. They seemed to have a good holiday and when they stopped coming to the bar, I assumed that they had gone back home.

A couple of days after this I was woken at about 3 o'clock in the morning by the sound of the phone ringing. I was not best pleased to be woken at such a stupid hour of the morning. When I picked up the phone I heard a desperate voice on the other end of the line:

'Kim, I need you to tell me the truth. Is Tania there with you?'

'What?' I said, still groggy with sleep. 'Who is this?'

'It's John,' came the reply.

'You what? Do you know what time it is?' I asked him. 'Is this some kind of an April fool joke?'

'No, it's not,' he said. 'Is Tania there with you? I need to know, because she has disappeared!'

9

Drawn into the Darkness

Is it not delightful to have friends coming from distant quarters?
Confucius

I was in a state of shock. It was 3 o'clock in the morning and John, who I had met just a few weeks earlier, was in hysterics, telling me that his wife had disappeared, and suggesting that she might be in bed with me right now.

'She's not here with me!' I said indignantly. 'As far as I was aware, she went back to the UK with you.'

'She did come back with me,' said John, 'but now I think she's returned to where we were on holiday. I know she's gone back to see someone, and you are the only bloke we got to know out there.'

'Well, she's not with me, mate,' I said, quite truthfully.

'I'm flying out there tomorrow anyway to try and find her,' said John, still very distressed.

'OK,' I said, 'you come out and stay with me and we will try to find her.' I hoped that the offer of accommodation would help to convince him that she wasn't staying with me.

The next day I met John at the airport. He was convinced that Tania had flown back out there and was even now shacked up with one of the guys she had met on holiday.

We got back to the flat and began to work out all of the places they had visited while they were there. We thought about the bars and restaurants that they had frequented, the people they had spoken to. The list wasn't that long, and at the top of it was a Turkish restaurant they had visited a couple of times for an evening meal.

That evening we paid the restaurant a visit – and sure enough, she was there in the restaurant, not even trying to hide herself. She had come back to start a relationship with the Turkish proprietor.

John confronted her, and they were having an animated conversation in the restaurant when the owner came out to see what was happening. Pretty soon he wanted to get involved in the argument, and some of the other Turkish staff were watching carefully to see how things developed. I left them to it and went out to give my Japanese friends a call. I wanted them to come over so that if there was any bother we would have a bit of extra muscle on our side.

After that I phoned my old friend Alberto in Barcelona. I knew that his uncle was a senior officer in the police in Majorca, and I thought it might be helpful to have a bit of law enforcement there as well. Alberto told his uncle to phone the police on the island, and they turned up just as things were beginning to get ugly. The Turks had taken exception to John coming into the restaurant and causing a scene. When the police arrived everyone settled down; they told Tania to go back with John and me. They also took her passport, and advised her that she should come to collect it the next day.

John was very grateful to me for my help. He was still very upset and very angry, and I think he would have beaten her when we got back to my flat if I had not stopped him. The next day they went to the police station to collect her passport, and then they flew back to England. A few weeks later I discovered that Tania had started legal proceedings to get divorced and had flown back to Majorca again. John had not bothered to try and claim her back a second time.

I decided that it was time to move on. I was weary of living and working with people who spoke a foreign language; I wanted to go somewhere where the people spoke English. I didn't want to go back to the USA so I ended up coming to the UK. I flew in and waited my turn in the immigration queue. I had to answer a few questions.

'What is the purpose of your visit to the UK, Mr Goh?'

'I'm here on holiday,' I said.

'How long are you going to be here on holiday?'

'About six months.'

'Who knows you in this country? Who can guarantee you?' asked the immigration officer. It was clear that this guy did not like me, and the feeling was mutual. I gave him John's contact details and said that he would vouch for me while I was in the UK. In fact I had a number of contacts in the UK, but I judged that John was the best one to give them.

Anyway, they allowed me in; and so I went straight up to London. I had a friend called Jimmy who told me that there was a part-time job going at a Chinese restaurant in the Kings Road. I presented myself to the owner, got the job, and worked hard. Pretty soon I was working there full time.

I had made a decision to try to go straight and keep out of the gangs. I wanted a new start and I wanted to earn some honest money; but the pay was poor and the proprietor kept the tips. Again I felt as though I had been unfairly treated. I had always thought that tips belong to the waiter (or waitress), and I still think that to this day. I did get to meet some famous people, although at the time I was ignorant of the fact. Cliff Richard had his Christmas party in the restaurant a couple of years running; I was serving him and I didn't even know who he was!

I also had a chance to do a big favour for a couple of my regulars. Bill and Lynne were loyal customers at the restaurant. I usually served them and I got to know them well over the months. On one occasion we were chatting after they had had their meal, and Bill said, 'We won't be here next week, Bobby. We're off to Sicily for a holiday.' (I had retained 'Bobby' as my English nickname.)

'Sounds nice,' I said. They were clearly very excited about their trip.

'You don't know any cheap hotels out there, do you?' Bill asked.

It was a reasonable question for him to ask. I had told them something of my travels – not everything, of course, but enough for them to think of me as a man with connections all over the place. I quite liked the idea that they could think of me this way; I enjoyed having that kind of reputation.

At the mention of Sicily I remembered the offer Mario had made me in Madrid. I still had a contact number for him and because I liked Bill and Lynne, I was more than happy to do them a favour.

'I tell you what,' I said, 'when you get to Sicily, you phone an associate of mine there and you tell him you are my good friend's son, and you ask him to help you find some accommodation.' I gave them the number and they went off on their holiday.

When Bill and Lynne arrived in Sicily, they phoned Mario as I had suggested, clearly hoping that he would give them some inside knowledge on the best places to stay on the island. In fact they got much more than they could have hoped for. First, Mario sent a big car to the airport to collect them. Then the car took them to a five-star hotel and when Mario joined them for dinner that evening, he said he would also pick up the bill for their stay. They were overjoyed. They were able to stay at the hotel for free, and Mario even organized for a chauffeur to take them sightseeing. They had a great time, and saved themselves a fortune in the process. I don't know whether they knew they were staying at this hotel courtesy of the Mafia. I think they must have had some idea.

At the end of their holiday, Mario met them before they left to come home. They were really happy, and very grateful to both Mario and me.

'I'm glad you guys had a good time,' Mario said to them. 'I want you to do one thing for me; I want you to take this back to Bob for me, please.' He handed Bill a matchbox with a small piece of opium in it.

'Tell him that if he likes it we can supply as much of that as he wants,' said Mario.

Well, they had had a wonderful time, and on the Saturday evening after they got back they came to the restaurant with a bottle of Chianti as a present for me – and this piece of opium.

'We had such a good time,' said Bill as he handed over the Chianti; 'thank you so much for the contact number, Bobby.' I was pleased to hear that things had gone well for them, and their happiness was there for all to see in the busy restaurant that night. In fact their enthusiasm had drawn some attention from the other customers, so there were quite a few eyes on Bill when he suddenly stood up and said, 'Oh yes! One more thing, Bobby. Your friend Mario gave me this to give to you. He says if you like it, he can get you as much of it as you want!' He handed me the matchbox.

'OK, thanks, Bill,' I said and pocketed the little box immediately. I think all of the other staff and quite a number of the customers were looking at us, and there was a noticeable lull in the conversation. One or two people made a point of looking away and whispering to each other. Bill sat down and smiled at me; I smiled back, knowing that most of the other waiters and a few of the customers would be able to guess what was in the box.

Some of the other staff teased me about it afterwards. 'We know what's in there,' they said. 'It's a piece of opium from your Sicilian friend. He's sending it over for you to try!' Most of them knew about my relationship with Mario. I did not respond to any of the comments. I was very embarrassed, although I didn't blame Bill and Lynne; they were young and naïve and they'd just had a great holiday. They wanted to make sure they did what they had been asked to do.

The whole episode was soon forgotten, and whilst I never got involved with Mario again, I did, of course, smoke the opium.

Generally I was unhappy at the restaurant because I was being swindled; in fact all the staff were being swindled. I started to get my own back in little ways – like drinking the boss's best wine. I was also eating my way through the stock of abalones, a very expensive kind of shellfish.

This was a bizarre time in my life. I was often in the local pub, where I became friendly with some of the local Irish community. Some of these people were paramilitaries, and one day someone offered me £500 to go to Ireland and shoot English soldiers. They thought my nationality would prevent me from being identified. I never knew whether this was a serious offer or not, but I had told plenty of people in the pub that I had practised shooting in the Singapore National Service and that I was a good shot. I gave the proposal a few seconds' consideration, but the stupidity of the thing put me off – the idea of Irish people killing other Irish people seemed totally crazy to me!

There were other temptations I found harder to resist. The boss had a number of antiques as part of the decoration in the restaurant, and I was tempted to steal them and sell them to supplement my income. I resisted that temptation. Then there was the boss's wife. She was a very beautiful woman, but not very bright – and not very discerning in her behaviour either. She liked me and she would often call after me, 'Bobby, Bobby! Come and see me.' I didn't want to know about her. I had been involved with a married woman before and it had caused me a lot of hurt; I wasn't going to go through that again.

Fortunately for me, a new opportunity presented itself before I got too depressed with the situation. A guy came to visit my boss one day at the restaurant and while he was there he introduced himself to me; his name was Martin Wang. He told me he was planning to open a new restaurant and he offered me a job there. This was a preliminary chat and he still needed to make some more arrangements, so I told him I was interested and we left it at that.

About a week later he called me and formally offered me the job. He promised more money than I was currently earning and opportunities to develop the business and take on more responsibilities. I agreed to the terms and went to work for Martin. Over the next seven years we built up the business from one restaurant to four, plus a Chinese supermarket.

I did not realize immediately that Martin was from a Christian family. His father was a pastor, and his sister was the Director of a Chinese Christian organization in the UK. I was not particularly fond of Christians at this time but we had a good business arrangement and I became the General Manager of the chain of restaurants. Martin paid me commission for getting more business and I was quite successful in that. My strategy for driving up business was simple; I would wine and dine the tour group reps and then arrange for them to have their groups come to my restaurants for a meal.

The strategy proved to be a success; we had Scandinavian, Spanish, German and Dutch visitors. The tour guide would book them all in to a London show and either before or after the show they all came to one of the restaurants for a Chinese meal.

Building on this success, I then got in touch with some big organizations that had their headquarters near one of our restaurants. One of my best customers was Rank Xerox. Often they would have Chinese delegations visiting for business and we would cook the food and take it to them at their premises.

Even back then a lot of companies did business with China, and because I spoke both Chinese and English, I was able to talk to all parties involved in the catering.

As the business expanded, Martin began to import other goods as well as the wholesale ingredients for the supermarket and the restaurants. We started to buy in Chinese calendars and other novelties that we could personalize and sell on to other restaurants in the area for use as advertising.

I continued to work for Martin and we were very successful in business. While I was working with him he provided accommodation for me, and it was only many years later that I discovered that a number of people in his family, including his father-in-law and mother-in-law, had been praying for me over this time. We have stayed in touch and now Martin is serving God by sponsoring the construction of schools and churches in communist China.

During this time I was doing well in my professional life, but my personal life was tainted with addiction. I was gambling heavily and flirting with the occult and black magic.

I continued to be involved with the triads, getting to know some of them through the restaurants; and I often went to gamble at their casinos. I was not working for the triads at this time, but their influence hung over me – relationships, gambling, money, reputation. I was only on the edge of the gang lifestyle but I was completely snared by it.

Beyond all that, I was hungry for something else. I had a need that could not be met by money or women or even prestige. I looked at Martin and his family and I could see the attraction of living a straight and respectable life. But then another part of me enjoyed the gang lifestyle. While I was in this state of confusion I met someone who seemed to be able to offer some answers. His name was Brian Templeton.

I was already interested in black magic and the occult, and when Brian started coming to one of the restaurants he and I got talking and I could see that he was very knowledgeable on this subject, and he had a range of connections with others involved in the occult. Brian would visit the restaurant with a variety of girlfriends; he and I would talk and they would sit there quietly while we chatted. Sometimes, if I got the chance, I would say a few words to them and try to get their contact details. If the opportunity presented itself I would even get in touch with them and arrange to spend the night with them.

Brian was a wealthy student of Richard Gardner, and a practising witch. He was part of a movement campaigning to see witchcraft revived in Britain in the twentieth century. Brian talked to me about his extensive circle of friends, even recommending that I go and spend time with one of them – a lady called Stella who was supposed to be the Queen of the Witches and who lived in the north of England. Intrigued by the offer and the chance to look at some rare books on the subject, I went to stay with Stella for a week. She ran a nursing home in Cumbria and the building looked like a castle. She owned a number of black cats and a big old house with a cellar that smelt like a dungeon. I listened to her teaching and I read her books, and I was both fascinated and unnerved by it all. Evil tends to be both attractive and repellent; but at this time in my life I was more interested in focusing on the attractions and tried to ignore the uneasy feelings.

I continued to read about the occult and meet up with a number of Brian's friends. Finally he invited me up to his club, near St Albans. Knowing the kind of money that Brian had, I decided that I would need to be very well dressed for the occasion. I had a good friend called Chris and I asked him to come with me as a bit of moral support. When the day arrived we hired some tuxedos, dressed ourselves up and drove up to the club.

When we arrived we were shocked to see people playing tennis completely naked. It was a mesmerizing sight. At first I thought we had come to the wrong place, but we had in fact got the location right. We had our dinner-jackets on, but we soon realized that everyone – and I mean everyone – in the place was naked. Brian, also naked, met us and got one of his guys to give us a room where we could strip off. I had never before walked into a bar to order a drink without a stitch of clothing on me, and I have never done it since.

When Brian came to my restaurant he would usually stay for a long time. He would arrive at about 6 p.m. with one of his girlfriends on his arm, and he would stay until 2 or 3 in the morning. During that time, when I was free, I would come and talk to him about black magic. Sometimes we would go on from the restaurant to Covent Garden for breakfast. He liked to tease his girl-friends by telling them I was a Chinese vampire. A few of them believed him and they would spend the evening sitting there, waiting to see if my fangs would grow.

I read all of the books Brian gave me and harboured an ambition to rise to the very top of the ranks of witches. I wanted to become a very powerful magician, not so that I could perform illusions, but so that I could have real power; I wanted to be like God.

Not everyone that Brian introduced to me made a good impression. One time he told me about a guy called Gerald who was an author of several books on black magic and the occult. Brian offered to introduce this guy to me, and I was keen to meet him; we met up at a restaurant and Gerald was there with a very beautiful woman. She certainly caught my attention more than Gerald did to start with. Gerald and Brian where chattering away as we had dinner, and meanwhile I was playing footsie with this girl. Everything was going fine until Gerald noticed what was happening.

'What are you doing?' he asked.

'Hey, take it easy,' I said, smiling. I had decided that I wasn't too impressed with this guy already, and I was not too worried what he thought; but Gerald got pretty upset about it.

'I'll put a curse on you!' he said, and in his anger he grabbed the salt-shaker off the table and began to tip the salt out onto the table-cloth in the shape of a pentagram. I looked on, faintly amused, as he went through the motions of putting this curse on me. When he was done I breathed out a long sigh and looked at him.

'Have you finished?' I said. 'Good. You know what? You are a charlatan, do you know that? You couldn't curse anyone if your life depended on it.'

He looked at me with a mixture of anger and astonishment; meanwhile my friend Brian was embarrassed by the whole thing.

'First of all,' I continued, 'you cannot curse people with salt. Salt is a pure substance – it wards off evil – so you cannot curse people with it. Second thing, I will show you how to curse people.' And with that I bit my finger so that it bled and then I used the blood to draw a pentagram on the table-cloth.

'This is how you curse, you curse with blood.' I was looking him in the eye now. 'You write books? You don't know anything. Get out of my sight!'

Gerald was about to answer me and continue the argument, but then he thought better of it. He stood up, threw his napkin on the table, grabbed the woman who was still looking at me, and dragged her out of the restaurant. As she brushed past me she whispered, 'Call me,' and then they left.

'Well,' said Brian when they had gone, 'you blew it.'

'I didn't blow it,' I said, laughing. 'You could see for yourself that this guy didn't know what he was talking about. This guy is a charlatan, he doesn't know anything. I am surprised you want to have anything to do with him, Brian.'

In the end Brian didn't argue with me; he knew it was true.

'OK,' he said. 'But there's someone I do want you to meet. There's this Scottish guy, he's a bit of an academic, and he's the world authority on voodoo music. His name is Alec McCloud.'

'Well, OK,' I said. I didn't sound too enthusiastic because I had never been that interested in anything to do with black people, and that included voodoo. It was just a symptom of the racist attitude that I used to have in those days.

I did see Gerald's girlfriend once. Although he thought I'd blown it, Brian was prepared to give me her number. I followed my usual routine: I saw her, I had her, and I was gone. I wasn't interested in getting involved in any long-term relationships at this time, and I think I did it just to make Gerald look even more foolish. As with all these things, the pleasure was temporary but the sense of unease lingered on afterwards.

I kept up my interest in the occult, because I was looking for the answer to a longing – a longing that I could not identify. I would tell myself that I was doing white magic, but it was all deception. The truth was that I was searching for something to ease the pain I felt inside me. I liked to think that any power I had, I could use for good, but really my motivations were all selfish: my reputation, my powers, my desires. I thought I would be a good witch or a good warlock, but I knew deep down that I would always put myself first. It was all a deception, and however much I tried to hide the fact, I was an angry and frustrated man, looking for an as yet unfound answer to the questions of life.

After leaving Martin's employment in 1981, I went up to Yorkshire to find my friend John. I also had a contact up there called Mr Ling. Mr Ling had been quite famous as a Pekingese chef at one of the big London restaurants. He had gone up to Leeds some years before to set up his own business and now I went up there to join him.

When I arrived I discovered that John's marriage had ended and he had now found a new girlfriend. He was about to move in with her and so he allowed me to stay in his council house in Armley near Leeds. I used the house as a base and put my name next to his on the rent book. Some time later I took his name off the rent book, so I had a rented house of my own! I started to meet with other people who had rented houses and I ended up with my name on their rent books. Eventually I had about four houses that I rented from the council, and I would rent them out to Chinese people who would come and stay temporarily.

I worked for Mr Ling and built up a reputation as a good restaurant manager; but as usual, I was soon bored. So in the spring of 1983 I made a decision. I would go back to London to re-join my old gang – not just as a casual player at the casinos, but as a full-time member.

10

Blood and Honour

Triads also use numeric codes to differentiate the ranks and positions inside a gang. For example, 426 would mean 'fighter' . . . Another code, 49 . . . would denote a rank-and-file member. 489 is the code for 'the mountain master' [Godfather], 438 for the 'deputy mountain master' [Deputy Godfather].

Wikipedia

Becoming an active member of the gang required a visit to see the 'Old Man' – the leader or 'Godfather'. So before I went back to the capital I had to take a trip to Wales to see the Godfather at his 'country residence'.

When I arrived I was taken into his office.

'So you want to come and work for me, eh, Kim?' he said after I had introduced myself.

'Yes, Godfather,' I replied, trying to show an appropriate degree of respect.

The Godfather looked at me with cold, impassive eyes; his face gave nothing away. I could not tell whether he wanted to employ me or shoot me.

'I have need of your talents,' he said, finally. 'We have a new venture starting in London and I shall be paying close attention to it. You and Billy will accompany me to London.'

And so I became a bodyguard to the Godfather, travelling with him, staying with him, and accepting that I might have to risk my life for him. As the Godfather had indicated, I would be sharing this responsibility with a guy called Billy.

Billy was a volatile character, always ready for a confrontation, always ready for a fight. It was inevitable that we would fall out occasionally, and one time we almost had a fight with each other. I was in a restaurant and some guy just came up to my table and started being rude to me; I didn't know why he was doing this or what had provoked him.

'What's your problem?' I asked, putting down my cutlery. He then proceeded to verbally abuse me, in front of the staff and customers in the restaurant.

'You,' I said, getting up and pointing my finger at him, 'you need to shut up or I will shut you up!'

He stormed off and I thought no more about it. What I didn't know was that he was a very good friend of Billy's, and he had gone straight to Billy to tell him how badly I had behaved. I was still in the restaurant when Billy turned up. He came straight to my table and stood over me.

'Why have you been rude to my friend, Bobby? What's been going on?' he said.

'It's none of your business,' I said to Billy, wiping my fingers on a napkin. 'He came to me and started abusing me, and I told him to shut up, because he needed to shut up.'

'What do you mean – it's none of my business!' shouted Billy, getting right in my face. 'I'm *making* it my business!'

'Calm down, Billy,' I said, 'this is not your problem.'

'You have made it my problem!' he replied. I think by this time everyone in the restaurant was looking at us. I knew that this behaviour was typical for Billy, who was always looking for a fight, always wanting to escalate a disagreement into a confrontation. I thought that we would now have to settle this with violence, but as I stood up to face him some of the Godfather's family came into the restaurant and asked us, with the Godfather's authority, to make peace. I think I was happier to do this than Billy was; he'd been spoiling for a fight.

Billy's passion for conflict was fuelled by the fact that he also liked to drink; and he would indulge both of these activities in the many pubs that he visited. On one occasion we were in London with the Godfather and, as usual, Billy had taken time out to go drinking.

The pub he chose was one often visited by some Vietnamese. The story I heard was that he had had a few drinks and then got into an argument with one of them, whom he proceeded to beat up. We never found out what the issue was, and it probably wasn't important anyway. The point was, these Vietnamese guys were upset, really upset; they left the pub, but Billy stayed there and carried on drinking, probably thinking they had gone home and that was the end of the matter.

The Vietnamese guys had indeed gone home, but only to pick up some knives. They came back to the pub again later that evening and found Billy still there drinking. They waited patiently until he went to the toilet in the pub and they followed him into the gents and stabbed him to death. No one else from our branch of the gang was with him at the time.

Later that evening someone put in a call to the Godfather to tell him what had happened. When he heard the story he was furious, as were the rest of the gang. What made it worse was the fact that these Vietnamese guys were actually part of our extended gang, and reported to another boss; they even knew

Billy, and that made the incident more difficult to resolve, more personal. The loss of a good henchman, and the loss of honour within the gang, left us all hungry with the desire for revenge.

The Godfather turned to the gang's 'Advisor' before making any further moves. The Advisor recommended caution and we were told not to take any action – for the moment. There would be police activity. The gambling dens would be raided, people would be questioned. We would need to make arrangements to be prepared for this.

Within a few days the police made some arrests and the people who had killed Billy were in custody awaiting trial. From our point of view honour would be restored if these men were convicted and imprisoned. Not that the gang would forget; we knew who had done this, and we knew that one day the murderers would be released from prison. It was possible that a few old scores would then be settled.

Although I did not talk about it with anyone, I was not surprised to hear that Billy had been murdered. He loved confrontation and he didn't care what anyone thought of him.

The death of Billy meant that I was now the personal bodyguard to the Godfather. Wherever he went, I went too; whatever was happening, it was my business to make sure that the Godfather was protected. The commitment was total – I would kill or be killed if that was required.

One of our main activities was to visit the illegal casinos. These casinos were run by Chinese people, for Chinese people. Other races, specifically whites and blacks, were not welcome. The Godfather employed gangs from the East End of London as doormen; they made sure that the ethnic origin of the customers was never compromised. Inside the casino there were no credit cards or cheques; everything was cash. The amounts changing hands ran to tens of thousands of pounds.

Occasionally the Godfather would send me out to collect money from people – the gang made a steady income from extortion. But most of the time I was at the Old Man's side, keeping a watch on what was going on. At the start of the week the Godfather rested at his home in Wales, but on a Thursday we would load up three cars and make the journey to London. We would stay in the capital until Sunday or Monday night. Over those three or four days the Godfather would visit the casinos, gamble, eat at the restaurants, engage in some business and spend some time with his mistress. Wherever he went, apart from his private room with his mistress, I was with him, protecting him.

Sometimes he would ask me to get some of the boys together so that we could beat some people up. Other times we would just show up and chat; the threat of force was always there and often it was just the threat of violence that got us what we wanted. Occasionally we were required to cause a disturbance in a restaurant somewhere, to drive home a point that the Godfather wanted to make to someone.

From time to time it was necessary to make contact with other gangs. The Godfather would ask us to make peace, or war, depending on what he saw as the best course of action for the gang. When circumstances required a fight, both gangs would get out the machetes. These fights were vicious, no-holds-barred affairs; I knew fellow gang members who died in some of these triad machete fights.

Sometimes diplomacy was the best approach. There was one incident where one of our lads got friendly with another gang and went and joined them. When the Old Man found out, he was furious; this represented tremendous loss of face for the gang.

The problem was compounded when this lad got some members of his new gang together and, knowing that the Godfather was in London, they went up to the Godfather's residence in Wales and beat up one of our boys who was minding the place. This was like a declaration of war; it was certainly the most serious breach of the principles of gang behaviour I had ever known.

The Old Man flew into a rage when he found out; it was worse than the incident with Billy. He gave everyone a call and gathered his troops together; we were all to leave London immediately. It did not matter what other duties the gang members were on – they responded to that call. So there were not just three or four car-loads of us this time; there were fifty or sixty gang members, machetes at the ready, heading down the M4 towards Cardiff.

We spent the next few days driving around the city, in daylight and darkness, looking for members of this rival gang. Immediately after the attack on the Godfather's home the other gang had gone into hiding. This was wise because if we had found any of them I am sure we would have killed them. I was now the Godfather's bodyguard and so I would be expected to set an example in this, and given the chance, I would have done just that.

After a week we received a message from this rival gang; they wanted to make peace and restore relations with us. The Old Man was still furious about what had happened, but he asked me to go down to Bristol, where the Godfather of this rival gang lived. One of our lads was based there, and he knew where their Godfather was based, and also where their casino was. But I was not sent down to Bristol to talk peace, I was sent to kill. I drove around Bristol for a week looking for their Godfather, ready with the gun that my Godfather had given me specifically to do this job. If I had found this man, I would have killed him or died in the attempt.

I returned to Wales after a week, unable to locate my victim. Meanwhile this rival gang contacted us again, and again they said they wanted to talk peace. They knew we had been looking for their gang members, and they knew that I had been dispatched to murder their Godfather. The problem was, the Old Man was in no mood to be reconciled and he did not release me from my mission; he still wanted this other Godfather dead. So off I went again, back to Bristol, gun in the glove compartment. Again I had no success in locating any of the members of this rival gang.

After a few more days we received a third message from this gang. Still they wanted to talk peace and negotiate a conclusion to the whole business. By now the Old Man had calmed down a bit, and so a meeting was arranged for the two Godfathers. The meeting was private, and I do not know what was said; but evidently honour was restored, because afterwards my Godfather released me from my mission and I returned to my usual duties. In the end this very serious dispute had been resolved without the need for any actual violence.

Bound up with the gang culture of violence was the need to maintain the honour of the gang and the personal respect of others. Like many of my peers, I would not stand by and see either my own name or my friends abused or insulted.

I was at a restaurant once, having a quiet meal with an elderly friend of mine, when a guy who I vaguely knew came in and walked up to our table. Now at six feet two, this bloke was much taller than me, and he was known to be a karate expert. He started arguing with me about a bit of business that we had been involved in and it quickly became clear that he wanted a fight.

The old guy who was with me stood up to try to make peace between us, but 'Karate Man' was not having any of it, and he pushed the old guy over onto the floor. Now one of my friends had been treated with gross disrespect, so I really got annoyed.

'Why did you do that?' I shouted. 'Why are you picking on this old man?'

'He's getting in the way, and my business is with you!'

The other customers in the restaurant looked on in fear and bewilderment as our confrontation quickly escalated into a stand-up row.

'Well, I'm telling you not to pick on my friend here!' I said. 'Tell you what, why don't you come outside and show me some of your karate moves, then!' And with that I took out my ice-pick that I happened to have with me. I don't know what the other customers thought, and at the time I didn't care.

Karate Man looked at the ice-pick, then at me, and then at the ice-pick again.

'Just run!' one of the other guys in the restaurant shouted, and Karate Man took his advice, running out of the door of the restaurant with me in hot pursuit. As I stepped out onto the street I could still see him running down the road, so I chased after him. I followed him all the way down Piccadilly past crowds of onlookers to the statue of Eros, waving my ice-pick at him.

I watched him as he ran into another restaurant where, once inside, he proceeded to hide under one of the tables. The restaurant belonged to a member of my gang, which was actually lucky for Karate Man, because I had to show respect to these folks. There were a number of my fellow gang members there, including the Godfather. They saw what was happening and came to pacify me, and to remind me that they did not want blood spilt in their restaurant. I took a deep breath and tried to calm down.

'You can come out,' I said to the guy hiding under the table. 'I am not going to hurt you, I promise.'

He knew that I was a man of my word and so he emerged and stood before me.

'I am sorry,' he said, 'for hitting your friend. It was most disrespectful.'

That was all I needed to hear; honour had been restored. I nodded an acknowledgement and he left the restaurant. From that day on he was timid with me and showed me the respect I felt I was owed. It was a satisfactory outcome to the whole matter.

Honour is critical to the culture and life of the gang. Once we were faced with a guy who had reneged on a business deal with the gang, and he became openly disrespectful to us. This guy owned a restaurant in Scotland and initially agreed to sell it to a member of the gang. Then he got a better offer and sold it to someone from a rival gang, bad-mouthing our gang in the process.

To be treated this way is a very serious matter, and the leadership of the gang decided to make an example of him. One gang member went to Scotland and murdered this guy. The killer was caught and imprisoned, but he was only carrying out orders from the leadership of the gang, restoring honour for us.

On another occasion, we fell out with a gang in Manchester. The dispute became a preoccupation for the Godfather because there was a lot of honour at stake. Eventually a group of the lads, some from the UK and some from Hong Kong, were sent to the restaurant where our rival gang leader often dined. It was a Sunday lunchtime, and the restaurant was very busy. The gang leader was there and, on our Godfather's orders, they slashed him and beat him up in front of the customers. The aim was not to hurt him so much as to shame him and make him lose face in the community.

Supporting each other was a central tenet of the gang. One day we heard that one of our boys who ran a restaurant in Cambridge was being harassed by some people. We took our machetes, got in the cars and made the journey up to Cambridge. We managed to locate the people who were harassing our brother, and we smacked them around a bit. There was no need for any real violence on this occasion – they got the message and there was no further trouble. For me this was business as usual.

During this time I had taken to drinking a lot as well as smoking. One day I went out drinking with some friends. We were trying to catch a bus in Oxford Street to get to Marble Arch. The bus was moving and I was the first person in the group. I managed to get on the bus but the others couldn't follow me. I went up the steps of the double decker to find a seat, and I didn't realize that this was one of those open-top tourist buses. When I sat down I realized that they had not got on the bus. I went to the back and looked out over the edge to see my friends chasing after me.

'We couldn't get on the bus!' they shouted. One of them was an older guy and he couldn't run so fast, and it was clear that they would not be able to catch up with me now.

'Don't worry,' I shouted down, 'I'll get off.' I was quite drunk at the time, so instead of climbing down the stairs and getting off, I just jumped from the top deck onto the road. I didn't know anything more until I woke up in Middlesex Hospital with stitches where I had hit the road with my head.

In those days I would get so drunk that I started to eat the glasses on the tables in restaurants. By the grace of God I never got cut; I don't know how. I look back now and I see God's hand protecting me at various times, even though I did some very stupid things.

In a restaurant I was once confronted by nine or ten members of another gang. They were showing me their machetes, but at the time I was not frightened. They poured me a glass of wine to goad me, but I just picked it up and crushed it in my hand.

'I don't drink with punks like you,' I said. 'You're not at my level.' Then I turned round and went back to my seat and carried on with my meal. I didn't even care whether they had the guts to take me on right there and then. As it happened, they didn't; they quietly left the restaurant and I was able to finish my meal in peace.

But in a deeper way I was not peaceful; I was at war with myself. I was drinking and smoking, using and threatening violence, gambling and womanizing – trying to fill the longing within me. I was turning more and more to the occult, to find that sense of peace that eluded me.

In reality, all of these things, including the practice of magic, stole my joy. The influence of black magic made me more chaotic, more restless, and more frustrated. I knew that I should be content; I had money, status, women, good food, and interesting friends. I had got to know one of Princess Diana's former psychiatrists; we talked about philosophy and the ultimate purpose of life. It was all part of me trying to fill the void in my being.

The conversations simply made that void grow larger and more urgent. I had moments of distraction, moments of happiness; but I had no peace, no joy. The only thing that seemed to be working well for me at the time was my career in the gang, and that became the fixed point in my life. Over the months I earned the respect of my peers. I was fearless and brash; I knew how to handle people and I was not afraid to look anyone in the eye and take them on. I knew when to use diplomacy and I knew when to use violence, and I was not afraid of either approach. Eventually my reputation came to the attention of the Godfather himself and one day he called me into his office.

'Kim,' he said, 'you have earned all of the respect that you get.'

'Yes,' I said. I knew that this was true.

'You are now my deputy.'

'Yes, Godfather,' I replied, bowing. This was an honour, but it was one that I had earned. The problem was the price I had had to pay for it. Now I was angrier, more restless, and more prone to violence than I had ever been in my entire life.

11

Sold Out by a Brother

I shall never betray my sworn brothers. If I break this oath I will be killed by five thunderbolts.

Triad oath

In the summer of 1985 my life changed forever. I was in Glasgow to collect some money. I did the job knowing that afterwards I would be able to relax and take a well-earned break for a few days with my new girlfriend, Karen. In contrast to my lifestyle, Karen was an honest girl who worked hard for the Inland Revenue. Her job was to visit the headquarters of large corporations who owed tax revenue and negotiate a figure for settlement.

I did the job in Glasgow with a minimum of fuss and boarded an overnight train for the journey back to London. From there I took a train down to Exeter where I had arranged to meet Karen. Everything went to plan: we met at the station in Exeter and drove on down to Exmouth and checked into a hotel there. We spent the evening together and I went to bed that night at the hotel more relaxed than I had been for a long while.

At about 6 o'clock in the morning, I was woken from what had been a restful sleep by our bedroom door swinging wide open. When I opened my eyes I saw two coppers and the hotel security guard staring at me.

'Get out of the bed, both of you,' said one of the coppers.

I blinked and got up. I didn't put up a fight because I had my girlfriend with me; it was not proper to fight in front of your woman. Also, if I had tried to fight, there would have been more trouble. Karen immediately started to panic; she had no idea what was going on.

'Oh God, Bobby,' she said, shivering and tearful, 'if I get into trouble I'll lose my job!'

'Don't worry,' I said, 'it's me they're after – you'll be fine. I'll deal with this – I'll tell them that you have nothing to do with it,' which was quite true.

They took us both to the local police station where we were questioned separately. I tried to help Karen out by telling them that she had nothing to do with any of my activities and was completely innocent. I had not told her about my past, about the gang and my activities within it. She was like an innocent bystander, and the police soon realized that they would not be able to get any useful information from her. In the afternoon they let her go, and I never saw her again.

They continued to hold me, of course. There were plenty of questions they wanted to ask me, and I soon realized that these weren't the local police; these boys had come down from Sheffield. I guessed this was because my only contact address was in that city.

'Tell us about Billy's death,' the first copper asked me.

'What do you want to know?'

'When did you first find out that Billy was dead?'

'A friend told me.'

'What friend?'

'Just someone I know.'

'Was it someone from the gang, or from another triad?'

I didn't answer that one.

'Who was it, Kim? What was his name?' There was no referring to me as 'Bobby' now.

'His name was Johnny.' It was an Anglicized name; I wasn't going to give them the proper names of any of my associates. The police continued with their interrogation.

'You're quite an important member of the gang, aren't you, Kim?'

'I have my place.'

'A place near the Godfather, eh? What do you do for him, Kim? What does he trust you with?'

Again I said nothing. The copper went on:

'Trust you with the bigger jobs, does he? So, for example, if he was owed some money, would you go and collect it for him?'

'I have my responsibilities.'

'I'm sure you do. What about if someone upsets your boss – what are your responsibilities then?'

'That depends.'

'What does it depend on, Kim?'

'On the circumstances.'

And so it went on. There were questions about Billy, about extortion, about the other triad members, and about relations with the other gangs. I told them nothing they did not already know.

The coppers questioned me for about an hour and then they put me in a car and took me up to Sheffield, where I spent the night in a police cell. I was in front of the magistrates' court by 10 a.m. the next day, and from there I was remanded in custody at Hull Prison.

Whilst I presented a calm exterior, on the inside I was furious. Someone had betrayed me, I was sure of it. How else could the police know that I would be in a hotel in Exmouth? I'd been in Glasgow just two days before! I had travelled all that way down south and they had found me. I was sure that this was an inside job and I intended to find out who had sold me. I guessed it was someone who wanted my position as Deputy Godfather in the gang.

This was my first experience in prison and I did not know what to expect. First they sent me to the prison doctor; I had a standard medical inspection, after which I was pronounced healthy enough to be in jail. Then I was taken to the stores, where I was given a uniform – pale shoes, socks, underwear, brown trousers, and a blue-and-white striped shirt. I had to take off all my clothing and accessories and put this on. I never got my watch or my pen back, or any of the other expensive stuff that I had with me when I was arrested. The only thing I had was the Giorgio Armani suit that I wore to go to the police station. That suit cost me £1,000, and I exchanged it for a faded and tatty uniform. I was just a remand prisoner now.

I did not feel humiliated; in fact, if anything, I felt a sense of anticipation and excitement. I thought about escaping; but I had no real enthusiasm for that. The main thing on my mind was anger, and revenge. I was definitely going to have my revenge. I also began to think about what I would say in the court, what I would say to the police, and what I would say in prison.

I was taken to a cell and I asked to see the probation officer. When he arrived I had my list of requirements ready.

'What do you want, Goh?' he asked. I was not used to being addressed in this way, but I was not going to have an argument with this man.

'I want you to phone this number.' I handed him a scrap of paper with a number on it. 'Speak to the guys there; tell them who I am and where I am. Ask them to come and see me this Saturday and bring the following items with them: 400 Marlboros, a portion of roast duck, a portion of special fried noodles, a portion of *dim sum*, some tobacco, some papers and matches, and some money – a few hundred pounds.'

I was allowed to ask for all of these things because I was on remand.

'Have you got that?' I asked him.

'Sure,' he laughed. 'These guys must be pretty good friends of yours.'

'These are my brothers,' I said, looking him in the eye. I was going to be the master of this situation and he was going to understand that.

I had an even more important reason for these guys to come in and see me, and I was not going to tell the probation officer about that. I wanted to give them some very specific instructions so that I could begin the task of finding out who had betrayed me.

On the Saturday the guys from Sheffield came and they brought all the things I had asked for. I had a good feast with my cell-mate, a guy called Thomas. In those days we were not allowed all kinds of electrical equipment in the cell, but we were allowed radios. I bought a red Roberts radio with £50 of the money the boys from Sheffield had given me, and I briefed them thoroughly on what I wanted them to do about this act of betrayal.

'What about the person who did this to you?' said Jackie, one of the boys who came to visit me. We chatted quietly so that the screws could not hear our conversation.

'What I want you to do,' I said, 'is this. I want you to go and find out who has betrayed me. I want their name, or names, if there is more than one of them.'

'What do you want us to do to them?' asked Jackie.

'Don't do anything – yet,' I said. 'Don't take any action on them until I give the word. What I do want you to do, though, is to make sure that the Godfather knows what has happened to me. When the time comes, those who have betrayed me will have their necks broken; they must be wheelchair-bound – you understand?' I looked at them and they all nodded, so I continued:

'When I know how long my sentence is going to be, I want you to go to each of these people once a month for every month of my sentence, and I want you to place a drop of acid on them. Just one drop is all they need, once a month, as a reminder to them of what they did to me. And I don't care where they end up, where they are in the world – you seek them out and you make them feel the acid, one drop a month. OK?'

The boys nodded and I felt a deep sense of satisfaction at being able to describe my plan to them.

On the Saturday evening the screw came round and said that if I was 'C. of E. or R.C.' I could go to the chapel in the morning.

'You want to go to chapel if you can,' said Thomas when the screw had gone.

'Why should I do that?' I asked. I had no interest in church or God. 'I'm not religious.'

'You don't go because you're religious!' said Thomas as if he were explaining something that was patently obvious, 'you go because it's another chance to get out of this damn cell, to get a change of scenery – know what I mean?'

I nodded; it seemed like a sensible move.

'And another thing,' continued Thomas. 'You want to volunteer to clean the shower-room; that way you can get out of the cell again for that job, and have a shower while you're there.' Again Thomas made it all seem so obvious; clearly he had been in this position several times before. I took his advice on both counts. I said I was 'C. of E.', even though I didn't know what that meant – but it sounded quite posh. I also volunteered to clean the showers.

Thomas was a gypsy, in his mid forties and a veteran of the penal system. He was a thief, and not a very good one at that, because he kept getting caught. He would tell me about the knuckle-fights that the gypsies used to organize behind the race-course at the end of the day at Doncaster. I had only been in the cell for three weeks when Thomas' court case came up and he was removed from the cell. As we said goodbye I wondered who my new cell-mate would be.

On the Sunday morning I attended the service in the prison chapel. There was a new chaplain starting there, a guy called Edward Ghinn. He was a young man and this was his first service. I arrived for what I hoped would be a pleasant change from the walls and smell of the cell. Edward smiled at me and gave me a prison Bible. The service started and Edward said his prayers and delivered his sermon. I did not take much notice, sitting towards the back, daydreaming and planning my revenge. The service ended and we stood up and sang the last hymn, 'Amazing Grace'. I quite enjoyed the melody, so that was probably the highlight of the service for me.

After the service I spoke to some of the other inmates about what I could do in the prison – I figured I was going to do a long stretch, so I needed to 'adapt to my environment', as my old insurance colleague George would have said.

'Nice hymn to finish with there, Vicar,' I said to Edward as we began to get ready to leave the chapel and go back to the cells.

'It's called "Amazing Grace",' said Edward. 'Did you like it, then?'

'Sure,' I said, looking around the chapel. I saw that to one side of the chapel there was a bookcase, and I asked if I could borrow a couple of books. I picked one and before I could choose a second, Edward was at my side, hurrying me out of the chapel.

'Can you hurry up with it, please, Kim – we need to clear the chapel,' he said.

Now, you need to appreciate that I had spent years in an environment where everyone was very sensitive about respect and honour. The way you addressed other people, and the way they addressed you, was very important. I was the Deputy Godfather, and that meant that I had commanded the respect of those around me. I felt that this guy, this white guy, was talking down to me, and I was not happy!

'I'm just choosing a second book, Vic,' I said, somewhat irritated. He left me alone for a few moments, and I was just choosing a second book when he came up and hurried me again!

'You know what, Vicar,' I said, 'you can take your book and shove it!'

He looked at me, astonished by my outburst. I was swearing and cursing at the guy as I walked out of the chapel.

I stomped back to the cell and I got my towel. I figured that a long shower might calm me down. I took my tobacco with me and headed for the shower-block. I could have a smoke while the other guys showered, and then I could take my time, have a good wash, clean the place up – just relax a bit and settle myself down.

I sat on the bench in the shower-room, fiddling with my tobacco and swearing at the vicar under my breath, the loutish shouts of the other inmates and the steam of the showers surrounding me.

As I sat muttering to myself, I got to thinking about how the vicar must work for the Bishop of Hull, so I swore at the Bishop for good measure. Still I didn't feel satisfied, so I thought about how the Bishop of Hull comes under the Archbishop of York, so I swore at the Archbishop of York. Then I really got in the mood. Thinking about this chain of command, I carried on muttering to myself:

'And . . . the Archbishop of Canterbury as well, because the Archbishop of York works for him! And the Pope! He can . . .' – and so it went on. In my ignorance, I thought the Archbishop of Canterbury must work for the Pope. Then I changed tack slightly and started to think about the fact that the Queen was the Defender of the Faith in this country. So I started to swear at the whole Royal Family, from the Queen to Prince Edward, making my way gradually and relentlessly to the highest authority I could think of – the Big Boss himself – God. Of course! God was the boss of all these people, and so I started to swear at God.

At that moment, as those stupid, careless words slipped from my mouth, I heard a voice:

Kim, why are you swearing at me?

I did not realize this was God. I thought to myself, *There's a b***** ventriloquist amongst the convicts!*

I was sitting in the big shower-room on a bench, smoking my roll-up when I heard this voice, and I thought that someone was fooling around with me. I looked around at the other inmates; the loutish grunts and shouts still echoed around the shower-block and none of the other lads were taking any notice of me at all. I scanned the room, looking for some sign of a smirk, some sign that any one of them was taking the mickey out of me – but I saw nothing.

It was clear that none of them were trying some 'voice of God' gag with me, and so I began to think that I had been daydreaming, that I had imagined the voice.

So I thought to myself: *I know what I'll do – I'll swear at God again.* And so I did. I started to speak out profanities against God, just as I had before; and as I started to speak, I heard the voice again:

Kim, why are you swearing at me? Was it me or was it the chaplain who was impatient with you?

It took me a couple of seconds to realize that I was on my knees. I had not imagined this voice, and I knew that this wasn't one of the inmates having a laugh at my expense.

Holy mackerel! I thought. *It's the chaplain's God speaking to me!*

I have never been so scared or so elated as I was at that moment. I felt God's presence, but I could not describe what was happening. For the second time in my life, I saw everything that I had ever done flashing in front of me. I could see the places I had visited, the people I had frightened, the women I had coupled with in a meaningless way, the violence, the shedding of blood. I saw the way I had conned people – some who I thought deserved it, and some who did not. I saw the bullying I had inflicted on others as a child in Singapore, the terrible legacy of my relationship with my father; I felt again the anger and fear, the lust for prestige, power, justification and honour.

And it all seemed like filthy rags as I knelt down in that shower-room. There were tears in my eyes for the first time since I had left home, since that time on the plane when I had watched my homeland race away from me. More and more tears came as I gained a true perspective on the way I had lived for the first thirty-six years of my life. I watched it all as if I was watching a film, and the sight of it made me feel sorry and ashamed.

But in the midst of the tears and the sense of shame, I realized that whatever I had been searching for all these years, I had now found it.

12

Under New Management

Amazing grace, how sweet the sound
That saved a wretch like me!
I once was lost, but now am found,
Was blind but now I see!

John Newton (1725–1807)

Now, at this time I didn't know anything about the Holy Spirit, but I knew that something strange was going on.

I felt an enormous sense of sorrow over my sins, but I also felt a sense of great happiness – a profound sense of release. I felt like God had taken all of the rubbish that had burdened me and lifted it away. This experience was not one I had been seeking. Moments before, I had been swearing and cursing every Christian I could think of. I did not even like the Vicar; I did not even like Christians! Yet here I was, experiencing the presence of the God of these people more powerfully than I had ever felt anything in my life! At the end of it all I heard God say:

Kim, I love you and I forgive you, but don't forget the consequences; the choice is yours.

So that was it. This awesome God was not going to force himself on me; it was up to me to come to him. And I decided to do just that – in the only way I knew how:

'OK, God,' I said, picking myself up off the shower-room floor, 'I will join your gang now.'

I was not going to mess around with something that was so powerful, so enormous; and no one had ever said they loved me before – no one! That was a first. This massive God loved me, and after all I had done! Besides which, I reasoned, it was not God's fault that the vicar had been impatient with me.

I was not alone in the shower-room, of course; and by now the other convicts had noticed my behaviour. Quite a number of them were watching me, amazed at my antics. Most of them thought I was having some kind of a fit. I was talking into thin air; I was in tears, on my knees on the floor.

A couple of them went off to get one of the screws, and when they came they thought I was putting it on, pretending to be mad for some devious reason of my own. Eventually I was taken before the governor.

'I have become one of you guys!' I said, smiling.

'Really? What do you mean by that?' asked the suspicious governor.

'I've turned to God; I am going to be serving in his gang from now on.'

The governor looked at me for a moment. 'Put him in isolation for a few days,' he said finally, 'that will sober him up.'

They all thought I was faking it for reasons of my own; none of them believed that I had had any kind of spiritual transformation.

* * * *

There are a number of reasons why prisoners get put into solitary confinement. Sometimes it is used to calm them down; for others it's a straightforward punishment for bad behaviour. For the addicts it's a brutal way of going through detox. But I wasn't doing drugs; if I was doing anything at all, it was the Holy Spirit, and no jail could separate me from him!

Conditions in solitary confinement were harsh and I was alone nearly all the time. The cell had a mattress and a bucket, but no other furniture or fittings. I was allowed out two times a day to empty my bucket, get some water for my washbowl, and collect my food. I got one hour of exercise per day. I had no contact with any other prisoners; I even had to collect my food on my own. And, of course, there were no privileges like a radio or cigarettes. I received no visitors.

But despite all this, I was having the time of my life! I was just talking and talking to God all the time and listening to him speak to me. He told me that I would not get deported because he had work for me to do in this country. He told me about some things in my life that needed to be sorted out. I realized as well that I needed to learn more about my new faith, so I had to get hold of a Bible.

I spent the most wonderful ten days of my life in solitary confinement. Every minute I was with my new-found God. We had such fellowship, I was bubbling with joy! I look back now, over twenty years later, and I can see that all the things God told me back then have come to pass, such is his faithfulness.

When they let me out, I felt as if I could not do anything until I had learned more about my new-found faith. I found the chaplain (as I discovered he was called) and told him about my conversion; and at my request he got me a Bible. I began reading it from the start, in Genesis; but I also jumped around to look at some of the other passages.

When I returned to my cell I discovered that the replacement for Thomas had arrived. My new cell-mate's name was Brian, and he quickly noticed my enthusiasm for the Bible.

'What you reading?' he asked me.

'It's the Bible!' I said joyfully.

'Oh,' said Brian. 'So you're one of them, are you?'

'One of them what?'

'You're one of those Christians, are you? What are you – Church of England? Roman Catholic?'

'I don't know,' I said. 'I guess I'm Church of England.'

Brian and I talked about my faith. His initial indifference began to wear away, and I told him that he should believe. I told him that God spoke to me, and was still speaking to me. During our conversation Brian broke down and cried. I think he became overwhelmed by the sadness of his own situation.

Brian's wife and daughters had left him because one of the daughters had accused him of molesting her. I told Brian I would pray for him. I didn't really know what else to say, but I was true to my word and prayed for Brian regularly.

Brian was due to move somewhere else in advance of his trial, but before he went he asked me to get him a Bible. I got in touch with the chaplain, who gave me another Bible – a King James Version this time – and I passed this on to Brian. I even offered to pay for it. I told Brian to read the Bible every day and I said God would help him. Brian was tried and, as far as I know, convicted, and was sent on to Armley.

So I got a new cell-mate called Terry. Terry was an older guy, in his late fifties or early sixties, and I could tell that he would have been well dressed on the outside – a very dapper bloke. He was always polite, often witty, always charming; what I would have called a ladies' con man. Terry and I were cell-mates up to the time of my trial.

I had been on remand for three months when my case came to court. I understand that, in all, there were 257 charges against me. The prosecution picked just eight of these as specimen charges, and the case proceeded on the basis of these.

I did not have much of a defence for the charges they had picked, and pretty quickly it was clear that I would be found guilty. When the evidence had been heard the jury filed out to consider their verdict. My thoughts were already turning to the length of the jail sentence I was going to receive rather than the verdict itself. Even my brief expected a guilty verdict. In the midst of it all I held onto the promise God had made to me.

The jury filed back in, the foreman stood, and to no one's surprise he repeated the word 'guilty' eight times, once for each charge. The verdict was delivered and I was required to stand before the judge.

I thought that God had promised me that I would be in prison for one year. The words 'one year' were going through my mind as the judge passed sentence. As I listened to the judge I thought he said, 'I sentence you for a year.'

This was exactly what God had said to me! I had a prison guard on either side of me and I turned to each of them.

'You hear that?' I said. 'God said I would be going down for a year and there it is – a year!'

'What are you on about, mate?' asked one of the guards, smirking.

'The judge has sent me down for a year,' I said. 'I knew it would be a year. God told me.'

'He's sent you down for *four years*,' the guard said, laughing, 'not *for a year*.' They were both laughing at me now; they must have thought I was an idiot.

'I don't believe it!' I said.

'Look,' said one of the guards, obtaining the papers from the court usher, 'look there – it says four years.'

I looked at the sentence on the paper, and they were right – it was four years.

'The judge must have made a mistake,' I said. 'I need to appeal.'

'Yeah, OK,' said one of the guards, and then they proceeded to take me back down to the cells.

When I got to Armley Prison, as a convict now rather than as a remand prisoner, I found out that Brian was there in the section for sex offenders. I would see him occasionally because I worked in the kitchens, and every time I did I said, 'Make sure you read your Bible.' I encouraged him to cry out to God and tell him that he wanted him.

Meanwhile, I instructed my barrister to lodge an appeal. I was told I had to wait six months. At the end of that time my appeal was heard and rejected. The judge who presided over the appeal said that my offences usually carried a life sentence and if it had been up to him, that's what I would have received. I was unhappy but undaunted; I had heard God say 'one year', and that was what I expected to serve.

I was keen to find out more about my faith. I had a probation officer called Mr Broadbent and I asked him to find me a member of the clergy who would look after me. On my behalf he approached some local ministers and asked if any of them would be happy to come and visit me. The first guy he asked turned him down, but then the second guy he talked to accepted the offer. His name was Mark Kellett. Mark had been an engineer in Singapore and when he found out I was from Singapore, he agreed to come into the prison and visit me. Mark started to come every month; he came along with a lady called Mary Pringle who was a member of his congregation, and who had a particular interest in visiting prisoners.

I looked forward to their visits and ended up writing to both of them. Although I did not know what was happening at the time, I realize now that Mark had started the process of discipling me, teaching me what it was to be a Christian and helping me to develop as a follower of Jesus. I told Mark and Mary about my concerns, the things I prayed about, and Mark advised me to join the prison Bible study. I also received visits from a Roman Catholic guy called Patrick Sheeshay. He was an elderly man, and he worked as a hospital porter. He would come and visit me and tell me his problems and I would listen to him, even though I was the inmate and he was the visitor!

I found that, as much as I was confiding in others, they were also confiding in me. In time I was advising the prison chaplain and some of the prison officers. These things happened naturally in conversation. One of the officers used to tease me by calling me 'Reverend' Kim, not realizing that one day I would have that title for real. Most of the other inmates were friendly and I got on well with them. I got a job in the kitchens organizing the distribution of food, reporting to the principal officer, and also to the head of the kitchen. Because of my reputation as a Christian, the head of the kitchen referred to himself as 'God' and to the principal officer as 'Jesus'.

My experience on the outside helped me to make a success of the job. I ran a very efficient kitchen for the prison while I was there. I made sure that everyone did what they were supposed to do and understood where they were meant to go. I knew which food needed to go out, where it was going and when it needed to be there. Generally the other inmates co-operated with me; all of them knew that there was no shortage of volunteers to work in the kitchen, and if anyone played up, another man could be found to take his place.

During this time I began to get the sense that God wanted me to work for him.

What a privilege! I thought. *This amazing God has turned my life around, and now he wants me to share that possibility with others.*

God is a God of possibilities and opportunities, and that is a very powerful message for people who are inside prison and maybe feel that there is nothing left for them in life. I knew then that I wanted to be an evangelist even though I had never heard the word.

During this time I clung onto the promise God had given me, that I would spend a year in jail and then I would be released. I decided to appeal again, and I had to wait another six months for my turn to come. In August 1986 the appeal was heard by a panel of three judges. By now I'd been either on remand or serving my sentence for about a year. The three judges decided that the sentence was harsh and they changed it from four years to three years. Because of my record of good behaviour I was given some remission, and the three years were reduced to one year. I had already served that, so I was expecting to be released immediately. The problem now was that I had to wait for another month to six weeks for the papers authorizing my release to come from the Home Office.

When those papers finally arrived, I was free to go. Not only that, but I was also given indefinite leave to remain in this country. Two of the key promises that God had made to me in solitary confinement had now come to pass. I was ready to leave prison and work out what God wanted me to do with the rest of my life.

13

Facing the Dragon

According to international police databanks and well-known specialists, the number of members of all triads worldwide will in 2007 reach almost 78,000,000, which is roughly equal to the population of Germany.   Wikipedia

You cannot serve two masters – I knew this. You can only ever belong to one gang, and I had chosen to join God's gang. So that meant that I had to leave my old gang, and that was not going to be easy. In the past I myself had punished others who had attempted to leave; now I was trying to do that myself.

I went to Wales to see the Godfather. We had not met or even spoken in over a year. I knew what might happen, but I was not afraid. When I arrived I was shown into the Godfather's office.

'I have joined another gang,' I said, jokingly.

The Godfather stared at me. I could see his jaw working and he was very angry, and probably confused as well. I had been his deputy and now I was telling him that I was deserting the gang. It was unheard of.

'I have joined the Christian gang,' I continued. 'I have become a Christian, and so I can no longer serve in your gang.'

The Godfather stared at me for a moment, beginning to comprehend what I had said.

'You know what, Kim,' he said, 'prison must have done something to your head. Now listen, if you want to work in London there is a place for you.'

'No, forget it,' I said. 'I can no longer work for you. If you want to make an issue of it, that's fine; you can kill me now and we can call it quits. But otherwise I am going to leave now and that will be it; our association is finished.'

He seemed to be weighing up his options. Should he kill me? Should he just let me go? Either option was perfectly possible. I pressed on with what I had to say:

'When you have made your decision, if you decide to let me go, just make sure you don't change your mind after I have gone, because if you come after me in the future, I will come back and kill every one of you. I shall come back and I will become the exterminator.'

Looking back now, I do not think this was a wise thing to say, and it was not a Christian thing to say; but I was young in the faith and I had been reading my Bible from the start, and so my mind was full of stories from the Old Testament, and principles from early Jewish times like 'an eye for an eye and a tooth for a tooth'. At the time this was all I knew.

'Get out,' said the Godfather, 'and never darken my door again.'

So I did just that. I went in there in the power of the Holy Spirit and I was praising God as I left. I think God's grace covered my foolishness that day.

And so by God's grace, from that day on I was able to lay down all of the involvement I'd had with the gang, with that culture and lifestyle. Since that time the gang has never bothered me and I have not bothered them. The old Godfather has died and a new one has taken

over, and the old gang and I have gone our separate
ways.

* * * *

When I came out of prison I joined Mark Kellett's
church: Victoria Road Methodist Church in Sheffield.
Quite early on, someone asked me if I would like to
bring some of the local Chinese people to church. So I
approached this in the way I had approached most
things in the past. I went to visit all of the Chinese people I could find and I simply said to them, 'You will
come to this church on Sunday, or I will sort you out –
do you understand?'

That Sunday there were a lot of Chinese people who
came to the church service. Afterwards the pastor asked
me how I had managed to get such a big crowd, so I told
him that I had threatened them with dire consequences
if they did not come.

'Well, Kim,' he said, 'as Christians we don't believe in
forcing people to come to church or threatening them;
it's all about choosing to be a disciple of Jesus, and
choosing to come to church.'

Having clarified my understanding, I went and told
the Chinese people that they only had to come along if
they wanted to; the following week some Chinese people still came but the crowd was smaller.

Mark advised me that I should be baptized by full
immersion as soon as possible to give a public demon-
stration of my new faith. The church did not have a bap-
tism pool but we were able to use the premises of a local
Baptist church for the service. It was a wonderful occasion, and an opportunity to bring the local Baptists and
Methodists together, and I started to have a relationship
with both of these church communities: the Methodists

because their church was where Mark was based, and the Baptists because they were close to where I lived.

Just occasionally I would see members of my old gang – if I was in a Chinese restaurant, for example. But now my focus was on learning more about my new faith and discovering what God wanted me to do with my life. Mark suggested that I should go to Cliff College for a year to learn more about my faith and to gain a firm grounding in my belief. Cliff is a Methodist training college with courses for people who want to be evangelists. It was this aspect of the college that attracted me.

I met Dr Bill Davis, Principal of Cliff College, in 1987 and he told me there would be no places available for that year. I was not put off; I wanted to go to Cliff and I would wait until the time was right.

In the meantime I used some of my contacts to get a job at a Chinese restaurant in Guernsey, and I left Sheffield for that job in 1987. I had a tough time in Guernsey; I was isolated from the church communities that had been looking after me and I found myself drifting away from God. I got involved with a woman and I could hear God telling me that this was not what he had in mind for me, but I thought I loved her. The tension between these two opposing forces made my life miserable.

Eventually, in 1988 I made a decision; I needed to leave Guernsey and pursue my ambition to go to Cliff College. I wanted to go there, and maybe I needed to go there to get my life back on track. At the interview I met Ron Abbot, the acting principal of the college. Ron was standing in for Dr Bill Davis (better known as 'Doc' to the students at Cliff) because Bill had been appointed President of the Methodist Conference that year. I was accepted onto the Leadership and Biblical Studies course, starting in the following academic year.

At Cliff there were a lot of new things to learn. I enjoyed going on mission with Revd Howard Mellor, Director of Evangelism. At the same time God was showing me a lot of things in my life that I needed to sort out; so I was being refined during this time as well as learning. I have found that this is true for most of the students at the college.

This was before the era of computers, so all essays and assignments had to be written on typewriters. I was learning about worship and preaching, the Old Testament and the New Testament, Hebrew and Greek. I went to a big mission in Southampton, as well as other missions in Warrington and Islington. The second-year students were leading us with a Cliff evangelist. My role was to knock on doors, talk to people, lead studies and prayer meetings, give my testimony, preach – basically everything and anything!

My involvement with missions work also brought me into contact with some old friends. On one occasion I was on mission in Islington with a group of Cliff students. I went to Pentonville Prison to preach, and I met Edward Ghinn, the chaplain from my days at Armley. He had moved on to become the chaplain at Pentonville. I reminded him of our incident in the chapel on my first Sunday in prison.

'I'd probably be even more rude to the prisoners now,' he said, laughing.

'Only if God tells you to be rude!' I replied.

One evening I took the team out for a meal at a Chinese restaurant. We went in and ordered our meals, and then a bottle of champagne was sent out to our table, compliments of the chef and owner.

'That's very nice,' I thought. 'I wonder why they did that?'

Apparently the chef had been peeping through the door, and he saw me and recognized me from the gang days. We also had a free meal that night!

On the same mission I took the leader, Paul Wakelam, out to China Town because he wanted to see the illegal gambling den. I took him for lunch – *dim sum* – at a Chinese restaurant. There were a lot of gang members in the restaurant having their lunch. Some of those who recognized me came over and introduced themselves, and then asked about Paul.

'He is the leader of the mission I am on,' I said. 'He is an evangelist from Cliff College.'

'Hi,' said Paul, 'I'm Kim's boss.'

Now he meant this as a joke; he was indeed my 'boss' on the mission, but the joke did not work for my former gang colleagues. As far as they were concerned, I was still their 'boss', and so there was no way that he, a white man, could be my boss. Paul did not realize the subtle cultural implications of what he had said, and I had to calm them down. He thought it was funny, but the gang members did not.

I also saw amazing examples of God's healing power on some of these missions. On one occasion I went to a pub called 'The Wheatsheaf' with my fellow student, Steve Richardson. The owner's name was Barry, and I could see that he had a swollen elbow. I felt the Lord speak to me:

Pray over this man's elbow for healing.

OK, I thought.

'Hey, Barry,' I asked, 'what happened to your elbow?'

'Don't ask,' said Barry, 'it's a nightmare! I got this wound from a piece of coral when I was on holiday diving in Australia. I've been on all kinds of medications, and it's still inflamed and it hurts like hell!'

'Can I pray for you, for healing?' I asked.

'Sure, if you want to,' said Barry; he had the look of a man who had tried everything else. I prayed over his elbow and went back to my drink.

A couple of weeks later we were in the same pub; Barry came over to us without me asking.

'Hey, I need to thank you!' he said. 'I'm healed now – look!' I looked at his arm and, indeed, it was no longer swollen.

'That evening after you prayed,' he said, 'a bit of the coral actually came out of my arm, and then the swelling went down, and now I am completely healed!'

I enjoyed my time at Cliff, and when I graduated with a certificate in Biblical Studies in 1990, I went on to join one of Rob Frost's 'Seed' teams. A Seed team was a group of Christians who went into an area in partnership with a local Methodist church. The church provided a house, we all got part-time jobs and earned the money to feed ourselves, and then we spent the rest of the time focused on getting a church plant going by engaging in evangelistic activity in the community. We were attached to a Methodist church in Wigan during this time, with the aim of gathering a new group of Christians who would become 'planted' as a new Methodist church. I served on the team from 1990 to 1991. While I was in Wigan I got to know a guy called John who was a fishmonger in Wigan market. He would use his stall to proclaim the gospel, putting up banners with messages like 'I will make you fishers of men'. John was full of life, a wonderful Godly man, and a master of market-trader's banter.

It was through John that I was introduced to the Full Gospel Businessman's Fellowship International (FGBM-FI). He invited me along, and so started an association that is still going, with opportunities for me to talk about my life and share the gospel – my favourite activity!

After my time with the Seed team I moved back to Sheffield, and my circle of Christian contacts began to grow. Over a period of time I had sensed God's calling on me to return to Sheffield to set up a restaurant and to use that as a base from which to proclaim the gospel.

So in 1991 I went into business with an old triad friend of mine, Mr Ong, who did not speak any English. I organized the installation of the catering equipment, all the fittings, and some of the wholesale supply of the food, and I was the manager and dealt with PR and solicitors – while he took on and managed the staff. Anything to do with English, I looked after; anything that could be done in Chinese was his department.

He agreed to let me use the restaurant for Christian work at lunchtimes, and so I invited various missionaries and preachers to come and visit the restaurant to speak to the customers. This programme was called 'Lunch and Listen'.

It was while I was working at the restaurant in Sheffield that God started to use me in the most amazing and disturbing way.

14

No Secrets from God

For God is greater than our hearts, and he knows everything.
1 John 3:20

God knows all our secrets; all of them. And what is really
frightening is that he sometimes lets other people know
our secrets so that we can learn from the experience.

There was a Christian couple who frequently came to
the restaurant, and one evening I got chatting to them.
They seemed like lovely people, and I knew from reputation that they were both well off and significant members of one of the church communities in the town. As I
was working in the restaurant one afternoon (that's generally a quiet period of the day), I sensed God speaking
to me about this couple:

Kim, you know Alan and Fiona?

'Yes, Lord.'

I want you to talk to them.

'Yes, Lord.'

*I want you to tell them that they are both committing adul-
tery and that they need to stop doing it; they both need to
repent and forgive each other.*

'Er . . .' My jaw dropped. I had only met them last
night – I had no clue about this! Also, I didn't have any

133

previous experience of hearing God on this level. This wasn't just me hearing God for myself; this was going to have big consequences for other people. And of course, if I was wrong, if this was not God at all, I was going to end up looking very foolish in front of paying customers – and good Christian paying customers, at that!

I decided to come to an arrangement with God:

'Lord, I'll tell you what I will do,' I said. 'If they call back, either one of them, I will tell them what you have said to me.' I knew that there was no reason why they should call the restaurant and I did not think that God would take me up on my offer.

Well, you should never give a bet to God. I was just making sure that the tables were ready for the evening trade when the intercom came on and I heard the waitress's voice:

'Kim, there's a phone call for you!'

I had to go down into the basement to take the call. The journey down three flights of steps felt particularly tiring that day; I just knew that it had to be either Fiona or Alan on the phone.

I picked up the receiver and heard Fiona's voice:

'Hello, Kim,' she said. 'I wanted to call to say how much we enjoyed our evening at the restaurant yesterday.'

'I'm glad you had a good time,' I said, my heart thumping in my chest. I was going to have to tell her what God had said to me.

'Anyway,' she continued, 'I told my brother about your restaurant when I saw him this morning, and now he wants to have dinner there with his fiancée this evening. Do you have any tables free?'

'Yes we do,' I said.

'Wonderful, and could I arrange for you to put a bottle of champagne on ice for them as well? You can put it on our bill the next time we have dinner there.'

'OK, I'll sort that out for you.' I was really struggling now.

'How are you?' she continued. 'Are you all right?'

'Yes, I'm OK,' I said, although she clearly didn't believe me – she could hear the agitation in my voice.

'Are you sure? What's wrong?' she said. 'You can tell me – we are brothers and sisters in Christ.'

'I'm fine,' I said, 'but there's something wrong with you.'

OK, I thought, *here we go*.

There was a pause. 'What's that, then?' she said.

'I was just having my quiet time, and the Holy Spirit said I should phone you or your husband and tell you both something. So now I am a bit apprehensive.'

'Well, what is it?'

'You're not going to like it,' I said.

'That's OK,' she said, 'tell me anyway.'

'OK, here goes.' I started to speak faster: 'The Lord says that your husband is committing adultery, and so are you, and the Lord wants you both to stop and repent and forgive each other.'

There was another pause, and then she said, 'Anything else?'

'No, but you both need to repent and forgive each other, if this is true.'

And at that moment I was convinced that I had got it all wrong. *Shucks*, I thought, *she's going to tell her husband and he's going to sue me, or he's going to come round and smack me, and now that I'm a Christian, I can't hit him back!* I was beginning to regret having said anything at all.

'OK,' she said, 'thank you.' And then she put the phone down.

That evening the brother and his fiancée did not turn up. The champagne was on ice in the fridge but they never came. I got on with my work but my mind was on

the conversation I had had with Fiona, and the consequences of what I had said.

At about 5.30 p.m. the next day I was having dinner at
the restaurant with the other staff. We always ate our
dinner early, before the evening shift started. There was
a knock at the door; and when I went to see who it was,
I found Alan and Fiona standing there.

'Sorry we're a bit early,' said Alan. 'Can we come in?
We need to talk to you.'

OK, I thought, *here goes. They're going to slap me with a
writ!*

'Can we find somewhere quiet?' said Fiona.

I took them to one corner of the restaurant. When we
were sitting down she said, 'Can we have a bottle of
champagne and three glasses?'

OK, I thought, *they're going to sweeten me up like the fat-
ted calf before they lay into me.* I was still convinced that
they were here to punish me for my foolishness.

So I found the champagne that we had arranged for
her brother, still cooling in the fridge. I came back with
the bottle and three glasses. When we were all sat down
again she turned to her husband.

'Alan, you tell him,' she said.

'No, you tell him,' said Alan.

'OK,' she said, and then she turned to me. 'You
remember you talked to me on the phone?'

'Yes,' I said, thinking, *As if I would forget!*

'Well,' she said, 'I waited until Alan was back from
work and then I confronted him with the accusation that
he was committing adultery.'

Alan picked up the story: 'I thought she had
been employing private detectives to follow me,' he
said.

Fiona continued: 'So I said, "No, the Chinaman at the
restaurant told me," and then Alan said, "How does he

know?" And I told him what you had said to me, that the Holy Spirit had spoken to you about it.'

I sat silently listening to the pair of them. Fiona continued:

'So then Alan said to me, "Well, he must be right, then." And then, after he had admitted to me that he was indeed having an affair, I confessed to him that I was having one as well. Anyway, we have done what you said we should do. We have both committed to stopping our respective affairs, we have both repented, and each of us has asked the other for forgiveness.'

What could I say? I was amazed that God had used me in this way and amazed that I'd actually got it right. Fiona and Alan were profoundly grateful to me. They had come along that evening to thank me. When they had finished their story they paid for the champagne, left me a £5 tip, and then they were gone. I did not hear from them for a while after that. When they contacted me again a few months later, it was to ask my permission to share the whole story with their cell group. I was happy to give them that permission.

This was the start of a period in my life when God was using me to speak particular truths to others. It was frightening and a privilege to be able to do this. God even asked me to speak to church leaders.

At this time I was friendly with a Baptist elder called Mike Allan. On one occasion I knew that Mike was preparing to go away for the weekend to preach. I was aware that he would be travelling on the Friday afternoon, and on the Thursday morning, God spoke to me:

Kim, I want you to go and tell Mike that when he goes to this place, the first person he meets is going to be called Jonathan, and Mike should say to Jonathan: 'Go forth and expand.'

I didn't really want to do this either, but by now I knew better than to try to resist God. I tried to call Mike but I could not get through. In fact I tried to call him several times, but I got no answer.

I went up to his house and got there at about 11 o'clock in the morning. I looked in the window and no one was on the phone, but when I called his house from a public call-box, the line was engaged! Eventually I went up to the house and rang the doorbell. Mike's wife Kes came to the door.

'Hello, Kim. How are you?'

'I am well, thank you. Can you tell me, was your phone engaged earlier, or is there a problem with it?' I asked.

'No, it's fine,' she said.

'Oh, OK. I'm here to see Mike,' I said.

She called Mike down; he was packing for his trip.

'Hi, Kim. What can I do for you?' said Mike, coming down the stairs.

'Hi, Mike,' I said. 'It's about you going away. God woke me up at 4 a.m. to tell me to give you a message. He says the first person you meet is going to be called Jonathan, and you should say to him, "Go forth and expand." It doesn't make sense to me, but I thought I should pass this on to you.'

'Well, it doesn't make sense,' said Mike, looking bemused, 'because the person I'm staying with is called Philip – he's the pastor there. Anyway, you've been obedient and given the message, so that's OK.'

I said my farewells and left Mike to get on with his packing, thinking no more about the whole incident.

A couple of weekends later Mike was preaching, and during the course of his sermon he talked about this incident.

'Kim told me that the Holy Spirit had told him that the first person I would meet on my trip would be a guy called Jonathan, and I was to say to him, "The Lord says go forth and expand." Well, I went to this place and I arrived at around 6 p.m. and a young man came to open the gate of the property.

'Well, this young man knew who I was, and he opened the gate and introduced himself as Jonathan, Philip's son. I was amazed, and I knew then without doubt that Kim's words had come from God. It turned out that Jonathan was only at the house to borrow his dad's electric drill, and so when I was settled in I shared this message from Kim with both father and son.

'Jonathan was overjoyed, and started to praise God. Apparently they had been praying about whether they should expand and church plant for the past six months. They had discussed the possibility of building another church at the other end of town and they had been unsure about this. Kim's message had given them the answer they needed.'

This was another confirmation to me that God was using me to speak specific words to specific people. You may wonder why God ensured that I gave the message in person, not over the phone. I have thought about this and the honest answer is – I don't know. I have learnt that the best way to work with God is to simply be obedient to him.

* * * *

I continued with my work at the restaurant over the winter months and into the spring of 1993. I had not seen Alan and Fiona for quite some time, but I was trying to organize a Christian breakfast event at the café and I wanted a speaker, so I decided to call Alan to see if he would be able to come and speak. We had a short conversation on the phone and he agreed to my request.

What I didn't realize was that, as he put the phone down, he turned to Fiona, who was with him, and she said, 'Who was that on the phone?'

'It was Kim, the Chinese guy from the restaurant.'

And before he could say anything else, she said, 'Oh, there he goes again! I suppose he told you that I've been committing adultery again. God must have told him!'

Of course, I had not said anything of the kind, but she confessed everything to Alan and concluded by saying, 'I think I had better pack my bag and go to my sister's or my mother's for a few days.'

It turned out that she had been having an affair with a guy who ran a New Age shop in the town – the guy she had been seeing before.

After this all came out, Alan called me again and asked if I would go and see him. I agreed and took a taxi over to his house. We talked about the issue and he told me everything, including how my innocent phone call had prompted a second confession from Fiona. I finished by praying with him.

I don't know what they did to resolve their differences, but about six months later I was at a FGBMFI dinner and they were both there. They thanked me for my honesty and support, and I told Fiona that I had had absolutely no clue about what she had been up to when I had phoned the second time. Still, God is God and he works out his purposes however he chooses to. The last I saw of Fiona and Alan, they were back with the Lord and together; and may God bless them!

It's an exciting and frightening thing to receive messages from the living God. These things always require a sacrifice on everyone's part, and the determination to take a risk. To be involved in this sort of ministry is to put reputation and relationships on the line.

On one occasion I was the visiting speaker at a FGBM-FI dinner, and as I was drawing my message to a close, I noticed a lady sitting in the audience. As I looked at her I heard the Lord speak to me:

Kim, that lady is going to leave her husband tonight and commit suicide.

I was really shocked. I could not get out of this one, or try to test it, or wait for someone else to act; I needed to deal with it immediately. I finished my talk and then, as soon as I could, I took the President of the Chapter to one side and spoke to him: 'I have got something very important that the Lord wants to sort out tonight.'

'OK,' he said. 'What is it?'

'You see that lady in the blue dress in the corner?' I said. I didn't point straight at her but I made sure that he knew who I was talking about. 'I believe the Lord is telling me that she is going to commit suicide tonight after the dinner. We need to speak to her; she is very unhappy in her marriage.'

The President stared at me for a couple of seconds and I watched as his face went white. 'That's my wife,' he said.

I was just glad that this was not the first time God had used me in this sort of situation. I don't think I would have coped as a novice. I brought them both together and we sat in a corner of the room and I said to her, 'You were contemplating suicide, weren't you?'

She admitted that this was the case.

I had a chat with them, and encouraged them to go home and talk and pray and give the whole matter over to God.

Another time I went with two Christian friends – a Baptist and a URC member – to visit a man who was wheelchair-bound. We had gone, of course, to pray for this guy, but then all three of us thought we had heard

God saying that I was going to be a minister in the Methodist Church, which at the time seemed most unlikely.

We then went on to pray for this guy and he got up out of his wheelchair, healed! I began to wonder whether the message about me working in the Methodist Church had some truth in it after all. God often used me to heal people during this time.

God also began to show me 'secret smokers' – people who would not admit to smoking but who did smoke. When I was able to identify these people I simply told them that they needed to give it up.

These were very encouraging and inspiring times for me. But perhaps the most precious moment for me personally was an occasion when I had a vision of Jesus. I was quite depressed and stressed at the time, and I had been praying, asking God to take away my depression. I was at a healing service and I was sat at the back, listening to the preacher, when suddenly I saw a very bright light – intensely bright, in fact – and it was coming up the aisle past the preacher and into the midst of the congregation. I saw this image, like the shape of a man, and he came to me and stretched out his hands, and put them on my head. At that moment I could feel the power and I also felt the depression just lifting off me. It was a most moving experience, akin to what I had felt in the shower-room in prison some years earlier. I could feel myself smiling on the inside.

Then the figure lifted his hands and he walked past me, and when I turned round there was nothing. I had not seen the face of this figure, but I knew that the depression had lifted immediately; it was now gone.

15

Marriage and Ministry

Where can I go from your Spirit?
Where can I flee from your presence?
If I go up to the heavens, you are there;
if I make my bed in the depths, you are there.

Psalm 139:7–8

During this time I was teaching at the local adult education centre. There was a steady demand for tuition in Chinese cooking. The course was very popular, so much so that when I was teaching it, my students kept asking me to devise a follow-on course. We would do a ten-week course, and then they would come back and ask for more lessons.

I thought about this, and I thought about the Alpha Course, and I began to wonder whether there was an opportunity here to get people to come to the church. The answer, when it came, was brilliant and simple.

I decided that I would devise a five-week course at the church for people who wanted to learn about Chinese cooking. I timed the course to run in the weeks preceding our Alpha Course, and I encouraged some people from the church to attend as well.

We had a good response and I had a mixture of Christians and non-Christians working and learning together. The course gave people who were not used to church a chance to befriend Christians in a church environment, but with some of the usual barriers removed.

At the end of the course I told the attendees that we were starting an Alpha Course the following week, and I would be cooking the first meal that evening, and the meal would include food that I had not taught them to cook on the course. This last piece of information usually piqued their curiosity, and so they would come along to the first week of the Alpha Course just to see what the food was.

My reputation for mixing cookery with evangelism spread and I received invitations to come and cook and speak at other churches. The usual format involved me giving a lesson in cooking a Chinese meal on a Saturday, and then giving my testimony; then on the Sunday I would preach at the church service. I worked on this format to make it as effective as possible and then I gave the whole event a name: I called it 'A Wok With God'. I have friends today who came to faith through this programme, like Mel Rogers, who retired early and sold his business so that he could open a drop-in centre for teenagers in his home town as a part of the Teen Challenge network.

As my ministry developed, so, much to my surprise, did the romantic side of my life. The first time I met Mary was at Cliff College. She had started work there in 1990 as a secretary to the principal, Dr Davies, replacing a lady who had gone out with her husband to work for a Christian charity called Mission Aviation Fellowship.

Things did not get off to a very promising start for Mary and me; during that first year at Cliff I decided that I did not really like her, and she did not really like me! She joined the choir and I was also in the choir, and when she came to her first practice I lent her a song-book because she did not have one. She took my book and forgot all about it, and I was not very happy with this! I went to the office where she worked and asked for my song-book back.

She gave the book back to me, and we started to talk and she told me she liked gardening. From then on I would go to the office from time to time and chat with her, just to be friendly. After a couple of weeks of this I felt God speaking to me:

Kim.

'Yes, Lord.'

You know Mary in the office?

'Yes, Lord.'

I want you to marry her.

Get lost! I thought.

I want you to marry her; I have chosen her for you.

Well, I was going to need a lot of persuading because I was still not interested, and I told God I did not want her. I had a girlfriend as a legacy of my time in Guernsey. She was a divorcee, and while I was still not happy about marrying a divorcee, I did love her and I would have married her.

But God wanted me to marry Mary.

Anyway, we still did not like each other very much when my time at Cliff finished and I left to join the Seed team. We were still friends, though, and from time to time she would come over to my house in Sheffield and have dinner with me. She was not very keen to make more of this relationship; and a number of people at Cliff were not convinced that I really was a reformed character, and they discouraged her from getting involved with me.

So we were in this strange situation where we would see each other from time to time and I would ask God if

I could just leave it and not get involved with her. And then God spoke to me:

You must persevere in this relationship. For this is how I show my love to my people. I do not give up, I persevere. You are showing her how much God loves everyone.

As usual, God was using my circumstances to teach me a lesson; maybe he was teaching both of us a lesson. Slowly, over a period of months, I began to learn the lesson, and I also began to love the woman.

While I was on the Seed team I went and bought a diamond ring. I had asked her what her finger-size was and she had told me, although I think we both still had doubts at that time. We had to break off our relationship a couple more times before we finally got together properly. Occasionally we would talk about what I had heard from God.

'God said I am to marry you,' I told her once.

'Well, he hasn't told me!' was her reply.

The irony is that it was she who proposed to me in the end! On 29 February 1992, we went out for dinner to an Italian restaurant in Sheffield and, taking advantage of the one day every four years when, traditionally, a woman can propose to a man, she asked me to marry her. I accepted her proposal, and a year later, in 1993, we were married.

The start of married life was also the moment for me to finish my association with the restaurant. When I came back from my honeymoon I found that my partner had filled the restaurant with all kinds of Buddhist idols; and at the same time I heard God speak to me:

Kim, now is the time to leave.

So I finished at the restaurant and took on the job of caretaker at Totley Rise Methodist Church. The job came with a house and so Mary and I moved in.

We discovered that marriage is a place where one can learn many lessons. In the early days of our lives together there were a lot of disputes and debates, but in the midst of it all I discovered that your spouse is the most precious gift God can give you in this life.

I discovered that I needed to love my wife as I loved the Lord. It was a lesson God showed me through some of the difficult times that we had together.

We learned how to live on a low income. I was on a minimal wage as the church caretaker, and Mary continued to work as a secretary at Cliff. I was happy enough to do this job while I thought this was where God wanted me to be, but over time I began to feel his prompting to consider ministry in the Methodist Church. I had not forgotten the words he had spoken to me when my friends and I had prayed for the man in the wheelchair.

I had not really considered the Methodist Church to be my natural home. I felt more comfortable with a Pentecostal approach, but I'd already learned that it is futile to resist the Lord. So I started by making some tentative enquires with my minister. Anyone who wants to go into ministry in the Methodist Church first has to become an accredited local preacher, after which they can receive a recommendation from their own church. Once this is done, the candidate's name goes to the Circuit, and then if they get through that phase, they will be considered for the ministry by the District. At the District level there is a panel of clergy and lay people who consider each prospective candidate.

In early 1995 I spoke to my minister about itinerant ministry and he was very supportive. Encouraged by this, he took my offer to the superintendent of the Circuit, and he also was very supportive. I began to believe that this really was a calling from God; I had heard him correctly, and he wanted me to be ordained for ministry in the Methodist Church. Again, I thought back to the occasion when I had prayed for the man in the wheelchair; it seemed that God was now confirming the things he had said to me on that occasion.

Full of hope, I took my request for ordination to the next level, the District. The panel considered my offer and, to my surprise and disappointment, they rejected me. The voting was three votes for my ordination, and ten against, and those ten included the chairman of the panel.

I was very upset. The panel said that they believed that I was not called to Methodism; rather, they recommended that I should go to a Pentecostal church and try my luck there. The problem was, I knew that God had asked me to offer myself for ministry in the Methodist Church, not a Pentecostal church, and by this stage in my life I was not interested in doing anything other than those things that God prompted me to do. I objected to the decision, as did my Minister and my Superintendent.

My case for ordination went to the Ministerial District Synod, a local gathering of ministers from the whole District. The Synod voted to overturn the District decision by a margin of 109 votes, and so my potential candidacy was back on track! I was delighted, and looked forward to making my case to the national body who would now decide my fate. This body, called the Connexion, was a panel of twenty-three clergy and lay people. At the end of their deliberations I went for a walk with one of these ministers, and he said to me:

'I must let you know, I don't like happy-clappy people. I will not be recommending you.'

I was stunned, not just by the rejection, but also by the insult that came with it. He was unhappy with my charismatic credentials and made it clear that that, of itself, was reason enough to reject me.

A week after this I got a letter advising me that I would not be recommended for ministry. The letter further advised me not to restart the process in the future. Amidst my frustration and disappointment, I assumed that the whole process was now at an end.

I turned to God and reminded him that I had been faithful to his requirements of me, and I now asked him to allow me to go and join a church where I would feel more at home. I heard no reply.

After the disappointment of the selection process, Mary encouraged me to think about going back to Cliff for a second and even a third year, so that I could build on my Certificate and obtain a Degree. The idea seemed good to me and so I arranged to get a student loan and planned to restart at Cliff in 1997.

During the course of my first term, in the run-up to Christmas 1997, I heard God speak to me again:

Kim.

'Yes, Lord.'

I want you to offer yourself for the Methodist ministry again.

Now I was really not happy!

'Oh no!' I said to God. 'Haven't I suffered enough for my sin? What more do I have to do? It's very painful even to think about it again. And didn't they say, "Don't call us, we'll call you"?'

I think by this time I knew that if God wanted me to offer myself again, I would do it, however unwilling I felt, and however hurt and upset by the process.

God kept on at me about this, so with something of a weary heart I offered myself again for ministry. There were different people at the Circuit and District levels this time, and when I presented myself to them, they all supported my candidacy without reservation!

A spell at Cliff College was then followed by a post-graduate diploma at Queen's College in Birmingham, and then another post-graduate diploma at Cliff College in Evangelism and Ministry. My first ministerial appointment was in Leeds, and now Mary and I are based near Loughborough.

During my time in Leeds, as well as ministry in the local church, I was privileged to serve as chaplain to the staff at the headquarters of ASDA. I was able to support customers and staff in a local store as well. I never needed to approach anyone; they came to me for counsel and prayer.

I applaud ASDA's vision in taking me on in this role, and I do wonder whether the success of the arrangement helped to persuade Wal-Mart, the US owners of ASDA, to start thinking about having a chaplaincy in their stores as well.

* * * *

I look back and I am amazed at how far I have come, by the grace of God. I owe my whole life to the Lord, who has such amazing love and grace for the lost souls in the world. And I am thankful to him for sending my wife Mary to share my life and ministry in his Kingdom. I am grateful to my wife for the long-suffering support she has given me. Thank you, Lord Jesus Christ, and also thank you, Mary, and all those who have journeyed with me in my life.

BIG BOYS DON'T CRY

Nick Battle

From humble beginnings, Nick Battle seemed to have it all. A successful career in the music business had brought rich rewards, working alongside such famous names as the Spice Girls, Michael Ball, Clannad and Simon Cowell.

Being married with two wonderful daughters had kept Nick pretty grounded, despite some of the temptations of show business. However, a traumatic family illness leaves Nick devastated. Can he cling on to any sense of meaning in life when his whole world starts falling apart?

ISBN: 978-1-86024-612-8

TAMING THE TIGER

Tony Anthony
with Angela Little

Tony Anthony knew no fear. Three-times World Kung Fu Champion, he was self-assured, powerful and at the pinnacle of his art. An extraordinary career awaited him. Working in the higher echelons of close protection security, he travelled the globe, guarding some of the world's wealthiest, most powerful and influential people.

From the depths of hell in Cyprus's notorious Nicosia Central Prison, all might have been lost, but for the visits of a stranger . . .

ISBN: 978-1-86024-418-0

ONCE AN ADDICT

Barry Woodward
with Andrew Chamberlain

Barry Woodward was a drug dealer and heroin addict who once lived on the notorious Bull Rings estate in the centre of Manchester.

Once an Addict describes Barry's descent into the murky underworld of drug dealing, addiction, crime and imprisonment, and gives insight in to the city's nightlife and music scene, which was part of his world. Illegal drug use claimed the lives of many such people, and it seemed inevitable that Barry would also succumb to the drastic consequences of his addiction. Then three extraordinary encounters changed his life forever . . .

ISBN: 978-1-86024-602-9

THE POWER &
THE GLORY

Arthur White & Martin Saunders

Arthur White had it all. Not only was he a successful businessman and happy family man – as a champion power lifter, he was literally on top of the world. But when he got to the top, he wasn't satisfied.

As he searched for a greater high, Arthur's life spiralled out of control. Drug addiction, an intense affair and a descent into violence followed, and before long death seemed like the only way out. As he stared into the abyss, an incredible encounter turned Arthur's life upside down. He would never be the same again . . .

ISBN: 978-1-86024-560-2